THE EXPERIMENTAL LITURGY BOOK

THE EXPERIMENTAL LITURGY BOOK

COLLECTED AND EDITED BY ROBERT F. HOEY, S.J.

HERDER AND HERDER

1969
HERDER AND HERDER NEW YORK
232 Madison Avenue, New York, N.Y. 10016

With Ecclesiastical Approbation

Library of Congress Catalog Card Number: 79-87757
© 1969 by Herder and Herder, Inc.
Manufactured in the United States

CONTENTS

GENERAL PLAN OF THE BOOK

FOREWORD

Blase Schauer, O.P.,
founder of the "Las Cruces
Experiment" in Liturgy

This book is a major breakthrough. Fr. Hoey, through his assiduous collecting and painstaking editing, has placed in our hands a good part of the rich variety of anaphora and new liturgical services that are once again available. The ice packs of centuries have been pierced.

At Trent the Church learned indeed how to "preserve" its heritage, but what was preserved was also put on ice and has remained frozen these four hundred years. The almost exclusive use of one language - Latin - provided a kind of formaldehyde base, and the variety of anaphora shriveled to one "Canon." Charism bowed to Legality.

Moreover, in the service of the Word, the Old Testament was barely given a nod, and the New Testament contracted to a very few formulae for categories - commons of saints and votive intentions. The unique personality of each day's saint hardly found support in any variety of scriptural pericopes. The saints were seldom seen as persons, but rather as categories. A painless "holiness for everyone" could be neatly described in universals. For this only a fraction of Scripture was desirable; and, as a result, repetition became the liturgy's inflexible mold. Inevitably, this familiarity bred contempt. The individual was forced to fantasize his private "holy" thoughts in his attempt to survive the monotony of a drone backdrop. The change to the vernacular could only intensify the anomaly.

Vatican II has given us a fairly clear mandate for expanding the potentialities of the scriptural word. With five Canons already officially approved, the door is open to the likelihood of a growing number for the future. Similarly, the repetitious use of Scripture in the service of the Word is already giving way to many new first and second readings never before heard. No longer are we going to be satisfied with arrangements of texts, either scriptural or non-scriptural, that are not evidently related. And if the celebration of the saints as heroes for Christians to remember is to endure, this can only happen if a theme meaningful to our present mentality can emerge. Momentous events of the past decades - incredibly diverse, horrendous, and thrilling - cry out for the flexible juxtaposition of the elements of celebration. We have learned that to celebrate means to confront the world as it is; that the liturgy must "celebrate" an assassination of a public personage as truly as it must celebrate a space voyage to the moon. Votive Masses can no longer be measured in tens, but in hundreds if not yet thousands.

Fr. Hoey's compilation gives us the best chance yet to appraise new events and to structure a service for them. In all likelihood it will also encourage further fruitful collaboration between poet and theologian. If we have stopped listening to the Word in solemn assembly, Fr. Hoey's efforts ought to be an encouraging "Ephphatha."

INTRODUCTION

"Even in the liturgy, the Church has no wish to impose a rigid uniformity in matters which do not involve the faith or the good of the whole community.....Provided that the substantial unity of the Roman Rite is maintained, the revisions of liturgical books would allow for legitimate variations and adaptations to different groups, regions, and peoples, especially in missions lands."

          - Vatican Council II: <u>Constitution</u> <u>on</u> <u>the</u> <u>Liturgy</u>, 37-38.

Gradually, since the close of Vatican II, official changes have been introduced into the liturgical worship of the Roman Rite of the Catholic Church: the Mass in the vernacular, permission for use of instruments other than the organ at the Mass, changes in the rituals of Sacraments, and most recently the introduction of a variety of Prefaces and Eucharistic Prayers (Canons).

Concurrent with this liturgical renewal has been a revival of interest in liturgical worship and in composing the types of different adaptations referred to in the above quotation from Vatican II's <u>Constitution on the Liturgy</u>. The purpose of this volume is to make available to all interested some of the experimental liturgical adaptations that have appeared, so that experts can evaluate them and point out what is good and what is not good. In selecting the items contained in this book from the many available, two basic norms were kept in mind: (1) liturgies that are worshipful and reverential, and (2) liturgies that are responsive to the needs of various congregations in our times. Although the selections made range widely in their individual quality, those farthest from the above norms were rejected.

This collection began about two years ago, on sheets of paper printed, mimeographed, Xeroxed, handwritten, taken from pages of periodicals, etc. As the collection grew, it was put first into a mimeographed booklet, then into a privately offset-printed format. This book is a substantial revision and expansion of the materials in the earlier forms and was compiled only after identification of each original source and permission to reprint; in addition, each item was restored to the wording that the original author wanted.

To bring the congregation into more active participation in the action called in the Roman Rite "my sacrifice and yours," each selection is keyed for dialogue recitation:

      <u>PC</u>   = Principal Celebrant;
      <u>CC</u>   = Concelebrant(s);
      <u>PC</u>,<u>CC</u> = Principal Celebrant and Concelebrant(s);
        <u>All</u>   = PC, CC, and/or Congregation

Not all will agree with the divisions made, or with the concept of such divisions. They are, in part, the work of the editor and are intended as suggestions only; therefore, they may be altered or disregarded completely, according to the norms of need and effectiveness in good liturgy.

As with any undertaking of such scope, this book was made possible by the cooperation of many people. Besides those named as sources of the materials contained herein, special thanks are due to the following:

Frs. Lawrence H. Jones, S.J., and James L. Empereur, S.J., for the items, sources, and insights they gave;

Fr. Gerald J. Sigler of the International Committee on English in the Liturgy, for tracing down hard-to-find sources painstakingly, patiently, and even joyfully;

Fr. Blase Schauer, O.P., whose "Laboratory For A Creative Liturgy" at the University of San Francisco in the summer of 1968 was an invaluable source of realization of the need and the norms for liturgical adaptation;

Fr. M. Benedict, O.C.S.O., of Our Lady of Guadalupe Trappist Abbey, Lafayette, Oregon, for help that only he and the editor can know;

Mrs. Louise M. Cooney, the editor's secretary, for unnumbered hours over a hot typewriter.

To name all would consume pages. God knows of their help, and He will give them their thanks, as I do prayerfully to Him.

Robert F. Hoey, S.J.

THE EXPERIMENTAL LITURGY BOOK

CALLS TO WORSHIP

CALLS TO WORSHIP

Note: It is presumed that any Eucharistic Celebration will follow a fairly standard outline; such an outline is in this book. Of the prayers in the one hundred series, some are suitable for more solemn occasions, others for more informal circumstances.
James L. Empereur, S.J.

---

101 CONTEMPORARY LITURGY, pp. 2, 3.

PC The Lord bless you.
All And give you peace.
PC Thanks be to God who sent us forth.
All He gathers his people again.
(next column)

PC Holy the God of Abraham
All and all generations to come.
PC The Lord has signed a Covenant
All and has sworn and will not change his mind.

All In his Name we were baptized to become one people in Christ.
In the water and the Word he led us to renounce evil.
From every race and nation he called and named his own.
We confess his holy Name in our doubt and in our faith.

PC Almighty God, who gave new birth by water and the Spirit, preserve you in his Covenant.
All Amen.

102

All Come, let us worship the Lord;
for he is our God and we are his people.

---

103 THE BOOK OF COMMON WORSHIP, Provisional Services, p. 24.

All Prepare our hearts, O Lord, to accept your Word.
Silence in us any voice but your own, that hearing,
we may also obey your will, through Jesus Christ our Lord.

104

All Draw near to God and he will draw near to you.
Humble yourselves before the Lord and he will exalt you.

---

105 A COMMUNION SERVICE, by Malcolm Boyd.

PC   Jesus, we are here for communion with you.

All   Jesus.

PC   Jesus, we are here in the imperfections of our shared and common priesthood. We are here in the ambiguities of our shared and common response to you, and the failures we have experienced in discipleship.

All   Jesus.

PC   Jesus, we would rather be selfishly alone with you than sharing with our brothers in your life. We would prefer to dictate who may or may not be in this circle. We would like to come here according to our own wishes instead of being obedient to you and the others.

All   Jesus.

PC   We have abused our lives and those of others. We have contributed to the breaking of our society and the fragmenting of our world. When we smile, our hearts ache. When we cry, we are ashamed for we do not understand our feelings. We stand close to one another in this circle and in life, yet we do not comprehend one another or ourselves or you.

All   Jesus.

PC   So we have gathered once again in this community.
We ask that we may hear and receive your Word.

All   Jesus.

PC   We ask that we may participate in the outward and visible signs and also in the inward and spiritual grace,
of communion with you.

All   Jesus.

....

PRAYERS FOR FORGIVENESS AND RECONCILIATION

PRAYERS FOR FORGIVENESS AND RECONCILIATION

Note: There seem to be two places in the Liturgical Celebration where a confession of sins could occur: one is here after the introduction to worship and before the readings; another (perhaps even more fitting) place would be after the readings, as the prayers of intercession before the preparation of the gifts. James L. Empereur, SJ

---

201   THE MASS REFORMED, by Roger P. Kuhn, p. 70.

PC   Let us confess our sins to God our merciful Father.

All   Almighty God, Father of our Savior Jesus Christ,
Maker of all things, Judge of all people,
we admit and confess our many sins
by which we have turned away from you and each other
in our thinking, speaking, and doing:
We have done the evil you forbid
and have not done the good you demand.
We do repent
and are really sorry for these our misdoings.
Have mercy on us, kind Father,
because of the obedience of our brother Jesus your Son.
Forgive us all that is past,
and with the power of the Holy Spirit
move us to serve you faithfully from now on,
setting our feet upon the new path of life
while building your kingdom here,
through Jesus Christ our Lord.

PC   The almighty and merciful God
has promised forgiveness of sins
to those who repent and turn to him:
May he move you to repentance with his Holy Spirit,
wipe out your sins,
and leading you to greater faith and obedience,
bring you to live with him forever,(+)
through Jesus Christ our Lord.

All   Amen.

---

202   VOTIVE MASS TO SEEK THE GRACE OF THE HOLY SPIRIT

All   Almighty God,
to whom all hearts are open,
all desires known,
and from whom no secrets are hid;

cleanse the thoughts of our hearts
by the inspiration of your Holy Spirit,
that we may perfectly love you,
and worthily glorify your holy name;
through Christ our Lord. Amen.

---

203   THE BOOK OF COMMON WORSHIP, Provisional Services, p. 38.

All   Father, we have done wrong;
by not caring when we should have loved;
by our indifference to the cry of need;
and by hating and ignoring our neighbors.
We have rejected the way of your Son,
and no longer deserve to be called your children.
O God, we cannot help ourselves; forgive us;
through Jesus Christ our Lord. Amen.

---

204   THE BOOK OF COMMON WORSHIP of the Church of South India, p. 7.

PC   Brothers, we have come together to hear God's most holy word,
and to receive the body and blood of the Lord.
Let us therefore examine ourselves in silence,
seeking God's grace that we may draw near to him,
with repentance and faith.
            (Pause for silent prayer.)
You who truly and earnestly repent of your sins,
and love your neighbors, and intend to lead a new life,
following the commandments of God
and walking henceforth in his holy ways,
make your humble confession to almighty God,
that you may be reconciled anew to him
through our Lord Jesus Christ.

All   Heavenly Father, we confess that we have sinned
against you and our neighbor.
We have walked in darkness rather than in light;
we have named the name of Christ,
but have not departed from iniquity.
Have mercy upon us, we beseech you.
For the sake of Jesus Christ forgive all our sins;
cleanse us by your Holy Spirit;
quicken our consciences;
and enable us to forgive others;
that we may henceforth serve you in newness of life,
to the glory of your holy name. Amen.

205

PC   I will arise and go to my father, and I will say to him,
"Father, I have sinned against heaven and before you;
I am no longer worthy to be called your son."

Let us examine ourselves in silence.
               (Pause for silent prayer.)
Let us humbly confess our sins to almighty God.

All   O God, our Father, we have sinned against you
in thought, word, and deed:
We have not loved you with all our heart;
We have not loved our neighbor as ourselves.
Have mercy upon us, we beseech you;
Cleanse us from our sins;
And help us to overcome our faults;
Through Jesus Christ our Lord. Amen.

PC   May the almighty and merciful Lord grant unto you
pardon and remission of all your sins,
time for amendment of life,
and the grace and comfort of the Holy Spirit.

All   Amen.

206

All   O Lord, have mercy on the sins of your servants.
May we banish from our minds all disunion and strife;
may our souls be cleansed from all hatred and malice
    towards others;
and may we receive the fellowship of the Holy Meal
in oneness of mind and peace with one another.

207

PC   Our help is in the name of the Lord.

All   Who made heaven and earth.

We confess to almighty God, our creator and redeemer,
that we have sinned in thought, word, and deed,
and that we were conceived and born in sin.
Therefore, we appeal to his endless mercy;
we seek grace and say:
Lord, be merciful to us, sinners.

PC May the merciful God have mercy on us,
forgive us our sins and give us the Holy Spirit,
that through him, we may fulfill his holy will,
and that we may obtain everlasting life.

All Amen.

---

208 THE BOOK OF COMMON WORSHIP, Provisional Services, pp. 22-23.

PC Let us confess our sins to God.

All Eternal God, our judge and redeemer;
we confess that we have tried to hide from you,
for we have done wrong.
We have lived for ourselves.
We have refused to shoulder the troubles of others,
and have turned from our neighbors.
We have ignored the pain of others,
and passed by the hungry, the poor, and the oppressed.
O God, in your great mercy,
forgive our sin and free us from our selfishness,
that we may choose your will and obey your commandments;
through Jesus Christ our Lord. Amen.

PC God shows his love for us, in that while we were yet sinners,
Christ died for us.
The mercy of the Lord is from everlasting to everlasting.
I declare unto you, in the name of Jesus Christ,
we are forgiven.

All Amen.

---

209 QUMRAN, MANUAL OF DISCIPLINE

PC Let us consider the goodness of God,
and our own lack of response:

All O God, we have acted perversely,
we have transgressed,
we have sinned,
we have done wickedly,
in that we have gone counter to the truth.
You have been right to bring your judgment upon us.
Nevertheless, you have always from ancient times
also bestowed your mercies upon us;
and so you will do for all time to come.

PC   May he bless you with all good
      and keep you from all evil,
      and illumine your heart with insight
      into the good things of life,
      and grace you with knowledge of things eternal,
      and lift up his gracious countenance towards you
      to grant you peace everlasting.

All   Amen.

---

210   THE LORD'S DAY SERVICE, pp. 8-9.

PC   Let us confess our sins to almighty God.

All   Gracious God, Father of our Lord Jesus Christ,
      who hast promised to receive us when we come to thee;
      we confess that we have sinned against thee
      in thought, word, and deed.
      We have disobeyed thy law
      and have not loved our neighbors.
      Forgive us, O God; free us from sin,
      and grant we may live and serve thee in newness of life;
      through Jesus Christ our Lord. Amen.

PC   Beloved, God has promised us his mercy,
      and in Christ Jesus has died for our sins
      that we may live in newness of life, obedient to his will.
      There is therefore now no condemnation
      for those who are in Christ Jesus.

---

211   A CONFESSION adapted from THE PRAYER OF MANASSEH,
      George Glanzman, S.J.

PC   Heavenly Father, Lord Almighty, God of Abraham and of his
          posterity in the faith,
      You made the heavens and the earth and all their adornment;
      Before your glorious majesty all creation stands in awe.
      You are God Most High, the Holy One of Israel,
      And your threat to sinners is unbearable.

      But I know that you are a God of compassion, long-suffering,
          most merciful.
      Your mercy cannot be measured nor searched out.
      You loved me so much that you sent your only Son to be
          my Savior;
      And you appointed him to be my advocate and intercessor.
      Father, in your mercy you have promised forgiveness to those
          who repent;

- 9 -

You have ordained repentance for sinners, that they may live,
and not die.

All   Heavenly Father, I am a sinner; I have sinned against you
and against my brothers.
       (Pause to consider our state before God and brothers.)
Now I bend the knee of my heart; I repent and ask for
your mercy.
I ask you, Father, to forgive me;
I ask you, my brothers, in the name of our Lord Jesus Christ
to forgive me and to pray for me.
Send me, Father, your Holy Spirit to guide me in all
your ways,
that I may praise you and serve you with joy all the days
of my life.

---

212   F. Michael Perko, S.J.

PC   As we prepare ourselves for this Eucharist,
let us confess to God and to each other
our faults against God and against our brothers.

All   With humble and repentant thought, Father,
we confess our sins to you.
We have failed to show your presence in our lives.
We have been indifferent to those whom you have placed
in our lives;
We have not accepted them as part of ourselves.
We have not tried to understand others and to become
one with them.
We have preferred ourselves to those around us;
We have taken and not given in return.
By sinning against them,
we have sinned against your body, the Church, and
against you.
       (Pause for silent prayer.)
Forgive us this lack of love in our lives
as you so often forgave it in those who were close to you.
Help us today and every day to live your presence
in our lives,
so that we may be reminders of you to those around us.
Give us the strength to love until it hurts
and then to keep loving
so that we may be one
even as you, your Son, and the Spirit are one.
Amen.

---

213 From "AN URBAN LITURGY OF IDENTITY," William Birmingham

PC Since we do not search your will,
All Forgive us, O Lord.

PC Since we are willful,
All Forgive us, O Lord.

PC Since we do not wish,
All Forgive us, O Lord.

PC When we fail to hate or love,
All Forgive us, O Lord.

PC When we choose hate over love,
All Forgive us, O Lord.

PC When we are so sure, we cannot doubt,
All Forgive us, O Lord.

PC When we are so doubtful, we cannot act,
All Forgive us, O Lord.

PC For being too involved,
All Forgive us, O Lord.

PC For remaining uncommitted,
All Forgive us, O Lord.

PC For forgiving our own wrongs,
All Forgive us, O Lord

PC For not forgiving those of others,
All Forgive us, O Lord.

PC For those we have excluded,
All Forgive us, O Lord.

PC For not caring about our world,
All Forgive us, O Lord.

PC For caring about our world,
All Forgive us, O Lord.

PC For what is in our hearts... (silence)
For what is not in our hearts... (silence)
For our sins against each other... (silence)
For our sins against all others... (silence)

All Forgive us, O Lord.

PC Forgive us, O Lord.

---

214 James K. Serrick, S.J.

PC O God, most merciful Father,

All we have come to confess our sinfulness before you,
before the whole court of heaven,
and before one another.

PC You remember that we are dust and you know our weakness.

All Have mercy on us, O Lord,
for we do not know how we stand before you,
whether guilty or innocent
in the scrutiny of your jealous love.

PC   We humbly bow before you and say: spare your people, Lord.

All   Purify our dedication to your service.
Remove the barriers that divide us,
the shortcomings that spring from our human weakness.

PC   Teach us to forgive and to bear with others
as you forgive and bear with us.

All   Let our hearts of stone become hearts of flesh
so that there may be no obstacle
to our love for you and for one another.

215

PC   Our Father, we stand before you,
as men, and yet as your sons --
in need of you.

'Father

All   You have chosen us,
Priest   and given us the wonders of human life.
You have loved us forever,
and shared with us your divine life.
And yet, we know we are still human;
we acknowledge our sin,
our sickening selfishness,
our refusal to love and to give.
We beg you now, as we approach your table,
to forgive us,
to give us new life,
to free us from all in our lives
that is less than human and Christian.
We beg forgiveness from all our brothers _And sisters_
whom we have used,
with whom we have not shared our love.
Our Father,
restore us to live,
make us new,
make all things new,
through Jesus Christ, your Son, our Lord. Amen.

- Brief silence +
- Absolution -given by Priest ....
- Sung Kyrie

HYMNS OF PRAISE

HYMNS OF PRAISE

Note: In the traditional Roman Liturgy a hymn of praise (the Gloria) is sung as part of the Entrance Rite. A hymn of praise, however, could be said at the very beginning of the liturgy, or after hearing the Word of God, or after partaking of Communion, or even at the conclusion of the liturgy. In some cases, the singing of a song could replace reciting a hymn of praise.
James L. Empereur, S.J.

---

301 Lawrence H. Jones, S.J.

PC Glory be to God on high:

All Peace on earth and God's good will to men.
We praise you, we bless you, we worship you, we glorify you.
We thank you for showing us your great glory.
For you alone are God: Father, Son, and Holy Spirit.
To you be honor and glory forever and ever. Amen.

---

302 THE BOOK OF COMMON WORSHIP of the Church
of South India, p. 6.

PC Worthy is the Lamb that has been slain to receive
the power and riches and wisdom and might
and honor and glory and blessing.

All Unto the Lamb be glory!

PC Unto him who sits on the throne, and unto the Lamb,
be the blessing and the honor and the glory
and the dominion forever and ever.

All Unto the Lamb be glory!

PC Worthy are you, for you were slain, and purchased
unto God with your blood men of every tribe and tongue
and people and nation.

All Unto the Lamb be glory!
Salvation unto our God
who sits on the throne, and unto the Lamb.
Blessing and glory and wisdom and thanksgiving
be unto our God forever and ever. Amen.

---

303 THE DAILY OFFICE, p. 310.

PC   Lord God Almighty, Father, Son and Holy Spirit:

All   We praise Thee for Thy revelation to us of love and mercy.
Three Persons, equal in power, majesty, and glory:
One God, which wert and art and evermore shalt be.
Blessed be the Holy Trinity and the undivided Unity:
Let us give glory to Him because He hath shown us His mercy.
Thou who art perfect in love and power and unity:
Keep us in fellowship with Thee eternally.
Holy, Holy, Holy, of whom and through whom and to whom
    are all things:
Bless us with thankful hearts;
Fill us with joyful hearts;
Save us with faithful hearts.

---

304 INTERDENOMINATIONAL COMMITTEE ON WORSHIP - draft translation(*).

Glory to God in heaven:
    peace and grace to his people on earth.

We praise you for your great glory,
we worship you, we give you thanks,
    Lord God, heavenly King,
    almighty God and Father.

Lord Jesus Christ, Lamb of God,
Lord God, only Son of the Father,
you take away the sin of the world:
    have mercy on us.
You sit at the right hand of the Father:
    hear our prayer.

You alone are the Holy One,
you alone are the Lord,
you alone are the Most High,
    Jesus Christ,
    with the Holy Spirit,
    in the glory of the Father. Amen.

(*) Reprinted by permission of the International Committee on English in the Liturgy, Inc.

---

305 THE MASS REFORMED, by Roger Kuhn, p. 66.

<u>PC</u>   Glory be to God on high.

<u>All</u>   and on earth his peace
to people in his favor!
We praise you;
we bless you;
we worship you;
we glorify you;
we thank you for showing us your great glory:
O Lord God,
King of heaven,
God the Father almighty!

O Lord Jesus Christ, only Son,
Lord God, Lamb of God, Son of the Father:
ridding the world of its sin, grant us your mercies;
ridding the world of its sin, accept our prayer;
sitting at the Father's right hand, grant us your mercies.

For you alone are the Holy One;
you alone are the Lord;
you alone are the Most High, Jesus Christ,
together with the Holy Spirit
in God the Father's glory! Amen.

....

STATEMENTS OF BELIEF

STATEMENTS OF BELIEF

Note: After hearing the Word of God, a traditional response is the profession of faith in that Word. Hence, different wordings of the traditional dogmas of the Christian faith are presented. James L. Empereur, SJ

401

PC   There is only one God:

All   I believe in him.

He is the mighty Father who made heaven and earth,
all we can see and all we cannot see.

He is Jesus Christ our Master, the Father's only Son,
generated before time began.
What Christ came from, he is:
God, the true God, and light.
He was not made but generated; he shares the Father's being.
For the sake of us men, to save us, he came down from heaven.
By the Holy Spirit's action and with Mary, the Virgin,
as his Mother, he became flesh and blood, a man.
For our sake, under the rule of Pilate, he was crucified,
he suffered death and was buried.
On the third day he rose from death,
as the holy books had promised.
He went up to heaven where now he sits with the Father.
He will come again in glory to judge those alive and those
    dead.
His reign will never end.

God is also the Holy Spirit, the Lord who gives life,
and whose origin is the Father and the Son.
We pay him, like them, supreme honor.
He spoke to us through the prophets.

There is only one true Church.
It is united, holy and universal;
the apostles' successors rule it.
There is only one Baptism that frees men from their sins.

I await the day when the dead will rise and a new world will
    begin.

All this I believe.

---

402   THE LORD'S DAY SERVICE, pp. 11-12.

PC   We believe in God,

All   the Eternal Spirit,
Father of our Lord Jesus Christ and our Father,
and to his deeds we testify:
>   He calls the worlds into being,
>   creates man in his own image
>   and sets before him the ways of life and death.
>   He seeks in holy love to save all people
>   from aimlessness and sin.
>   He judges men and nations by his righteous will
>   declared through prophets and apostles.
(We believe) in Jesus Christ, the man of Nazareth,
our crucified and risen Lord;
>   He has come to us
>   and shared our common lot,
>   conquering sin and death
>   and reconciling the world to himself.
He bestows upon us his Holy Spirit,
>   creating and renewing the church of Jesus Christ,
>   binding in covenant faithful people of all ages,
>   tongues, and races.
He calls us into his church
>   to accept the cost and joy of discipleship,
>   to be his servants in the service of men,
>   to proclaim the gospel to all the world
>   and resist the powers of evil,
>   to share in Christ's baptism and eat at his table.
>   to join him in his passion and victory.
He promises to all who trust him
>   forgiveness of sins and fullness of grace,
>   courage in the struggle for justice and peace,
>   his presence in trial and rejoicing,
>   and eternal life in his kingdom which has no end.
Blessing and honor, glory and power be unto him.   Amen.

---

403   Interdenominational Committee on Worship - draft translation
of the Nicene Creed(*).

We believe in one God, the Father, the Almighty,
maker of heaven and earth,
of all things visible and invisible.

We believe in the one Lord, Jesus Christ,
the only-begotten Son of God,
God from God(#), Light from Light, true God from true God,
begotten, not made, one in being (##) with the Father.
Through him all things were made.

For us men and for our salvation
    he came down from heaven;
    by the power of the Holy Spirit
    he was born of the Virgin Mary, and became man.
For our sake he was crucified under Pontius Pilate;
    he suffered, died, and was buried.
He arose on the third day
    in fulfillment of the Scriptures.
He entered into heaven
    and is seated at the right hand of the Father.
He will come again in glory to judge the living and the dead,
    and his kingdom will have no end.

We believe in the Holy Spirit, the Lord, the giver of life;
    who proceeds from the Father (and the Son).
    Together with the Father and the Son he is worshipped and
        glorified.
He has spoken through the prophets.
We believe in one, holy, catholic, and apostolic Church.
We acknowledge one baptism for the forgiveness of sins.
We look for the resurrection of the dead,
    and the life of the world to come. Amen.

(*)   Reprinted by permission of the International Committee on Eng-
        lish in the Liturgy, Inc.

(#)   Suggested that serious consideration be given towards omitting
        this phrase in future rendering.
(##) "Divine being" also suggested.

---

404 CONTEMPORARY LITURGY, p. 3.

PC   We believe in one God, and, led by his Spirit,
      know him in his Son.

All   We confess you, O Father, and your love for the world,
          by whose hand creation is, and change and rest are given.
      We confess you, Jesus Christ, Son of God, Son of Mary,
          who suffered death on the cross, and was raised to set
              men free;
          by whom we know the Father.
      We confess you, Holy Spirit, who calls, forgives,
          and gathers the faithful into one Church,
          to serve you with thanksgiving, unto the New Life
              to come.
      Father, Son, Holy Spirit, in you do we trust. Amen.

PC   In the Father almighty,
       Creator of the heavens and the earth;

       And in Jesus Christ, his only Son our Lord,
       who was conceived by the Holy Spirit,
           born to Mary, a virgin,
           tortured under Pontius Pilate,
           crucified, killed, and buried,
           sinking down among the dead;
           and after rising from the dead on the third day
           and going up into the heavens,
           sits at the right hand of God the Father almighty:
           and will come from there to judge the
           living and the dead;

       I put my faith in the Holy Spirit,
       the holy and catholic Church,
       the fellowship of the saints,
       the forgiveness of our sins,
       the rising of our bodies
       and our living with God forever.
       Amen.

Or else the following:

PC   Hear, O Israel!
       the Lord is our God,
       the Lord alone!

All   I will love the Lord, my God,
       with all my heart,
       and with all my soul,
       and with all my might;
       and I will love my neighbor as myself:
       All that the Lord has said, we will heed and do,
       (+) in the name of the Father and of the Son
       and of the Holy Spirit. Amen.

....

OFFERING OF THE GIFTS

OFFERING OF THE GIFTS

Note: The procedure of the presentation of gifts could vary
widely with different groups: hymns, a procession, prayers; and in
some circumstances the whole ceremony could be expressed with a
gesture unaccompanied by words.
Rev. James L. Empereur, SJ

501 THE BOOK OF COMMON WORSHIP of the Church of
South India, p. 14.

PC Behold, how good and joyful a thing it is, brothers,
to dwell together in unity;
We, who are many, are one bread, one body,
for we all partake of the one bread.

All I will offer in his dwelling an oblation with great
gladness;
I will sing and speak praises unto the Lord.

PC Holy Father, who through the blood of your dear Son
have consecrated for us a new and living way to your throne
of grace,
we come to you through him, unworthy as we are,
and we humbly beseech you to accept and use us and these our
gifts for your glory.
All that is in heaven and earth is yours,
and of your own do we give you.

All Amen.
Be present, be present, O Jesus, High-Priest,
as you were in the midst of your disciples,
and make yourself known to us in the breaking of the bread,
who live and reign with the Father and the Holy Spirit,
one God, for ever and ever. Amen.

---

502 THE LORD'S DAY SERVICE, pp. 15-16.

PC Luke the Evangelist records that
on the evening of the first day of the week,
the same day on which our Lord rose from the dead,
when he was at table with them,
he took bread and blessed and broke it, and gave it to them,
and their eyes were opened and they knew him.

All Beloved, this is the joyful feast of the people of God.
Come from the East and the West, from the North and the
South, and gather about the Table of the Lord.

503

PC   Almighty God, you have set a table before us
and have called us to feast with you.

All   Prepare us in mind and spirit,
that we may prepare this Eucharist in your name
and bring honor to your Son, our Savior, Jesus Christ.

---

504 CONTEMPORARY LITURGY, pp. 4-5.

PC   Worthy are you, our Lord and God,
to receive honor, thanks, and praise,
for by your will were all things made.

All   Look with favor, O Lord,
Upon this world, its nations and cultures,
homes and schools, arts, commerce and industry,
the occupations and leisure of all.

Look with mercy, O Christ,
upon all men and every human need,
the joy and triumph, conflict and failure,
the anxiety, fear, hate and despair.

Look with favor, O Lord,
upon your whole Church and all her faithful,
upon their holy vocation of work and prayer,
upon us who offer, and these our gifts.

PC   O Lord, God, heavenly Father, bless this bread and wine
all our gifts, and us, that we may celebrate
this Eucharist with joy.

---

505 John L'Heureux, S.J.

PC   (while pouring wine and water:)
O God, you wonderfully ennobled human nature in creating it
and even more so in renewing it.
We ask that through the mystery of this bread and wine,
we may share his divinity, who has shared our humanity,
Jesus Christ, your Son our Lord, who lives and reigns with
you in the unity of the Holy Spirit, God.

All   Amen.

PC   (while elevating the paten and chalice:)
Almighty Father, we offer you this bread and wine
which we will consecrate the body and blood of your Son,
    Jesus Christ,
to the honor of your name.

All   Amen.

506

PC   Be pleased to accept,
O Holy Father, almighty and eternal God,
this offering of bread and wine
which we, your unworthy but willing servants, make to you,
on behalf of your holy Church,
for all believers and unbelievers living and dead,
that it may preserve us for everlasting life
in union with you,
and be for us a source of strength
joyfully to carry out the work which you have given us
to accomplish in this world.
We ask this in the name of our Lord Jesus Christ,
whose Body and Blood this offering is to become,
who offered and continues to offer himself
in this sacrifice for us, your children,
and who lives and reigns with you in the unity
of the Holy Spirit as God for ever.

All   Amen.

---

507   Louis M. Savary, S.J.

PC   Holy Father, we present to you this bread and wine,
trusting that your life-giving kindness will forgive
    our failures in love.
We hope this offering will please you
and bring salvation to us and to all men.

All   Lord Jesus, sincerely we ask you to accept us with
    the offerings we present today.
Holy Spirit, come and bless this bread and wine prepared
    in your honor.

....

PREFACES

PREFACES

Note: Originally a part of the Eucharistic Prayer proper, the paean of praise offered by all creation to God has become, in the course of time, an introduction to the core of the Mass. Besides those below, other examples of experimental Prefaces will be found in the sections of Eucharistic Prayers and of Complete Liturgies.

---

551   George Glanzman, S.J.

PC   We praise you and we thank you, almighty God,
    our Maker and our Father,
    through Jesus Christ, your Son.
You who made the heavens and the earth have made us men to
    be a statue of yourself;
    you have given us glory and honor and set us a little
    lower than yourself.
In your gracious love you have chosen us and offered us your
    covenant;
    we are your people and you are our God.
You have raised us above our creaturehood and rescued us
    from our slavery to sin through the life, death, res-
    urrection, and glorious enthronement of your own Son.
You have poured out your Holy Spirit upon us,
    and sealed us as yours now and for eternity.
Though we are unworthy, you invite us to join your heavenly
    court in praise and adoration of you, as we say:

All   Holy, Holy, Holy,.....

---

552   UNITY PREFACE, F. Michael Perko, S.J.

PC   We give you thanks, Father, for all you have given us.

We thank you for the joy of living,
    for the love and understanding which we receive
    and so are able to give.
We thank you for all the material benefits
    with which you have given peace and joy to our lives,
    and which you have meant us to share.

We thank you for our oneness.

You have given us the world as a sign
    of the oneness of all creation.
You have given us the Church as a sign
    of the oneness of all who believe.

You have given us each other as a sign
of the beauty and joy of human oneness.

But most important, Father,
you have given us this Eucharist as an ever-present sign
of the oneness in you
and of our union together in Christ your Son
who is himself one with you and the Spirit.

Gathering together as one community,
we join all visible and invisible creation
in praise of your divine oneness,
saying:

All   Holy, Holy, Holy.....

---

553   WITNESS PREFACE, F. Michael Perko, S.J.

PC   Today and every day we offer you thanks, Father,
for the gifts of life and of love,
hope and joy,
peace and consolation
which you have given us.

We thank you for your earthly blessings:
for food and drink,
shelter and warmth
and blessings of a free land.

We thank you, Father, for the witness of your love
which has been shown to us in many ways.
We have seen it in the lives of those around us.
We have seen it in the courage of such men as those
whose feast we celebrate today.
We have seen it in the Church, the sacrament
of your presence in the world.

But most of all, Father, we have seen it
in the example of Christ your Son,
in whom we have all found a new life
and the courage to witness to your love.

In praise of this same Great Witness to your love,
we join together as a community
with all of your people,
and say:

All   Holy, Holy, Holy.....

---

554 BAROQUE MOMENT: Preface of Christ the Worker,
by Francis W. Sweeney, S.J.

PC Just it is and meet and truly right
And credit in the ledger of salvation
That all our thoughts hark back upon His praise
That every cup we lift should toast His love
And every loaf we break remembrance Him
Who gave His flesh like bread to feed the world
Because from word to flesh, from flesh to bread
The faith, His gift, bears reason like a child.
And as the life of taxes, trams and tea
Goes witless if we turn from witnesses,
We build the white, just city of our hope
Upon the promise of a carpenter.
And from this island of our exile chime
Our Sanctus with the arrow-agile choirs
And hand and wing are lifted to our Lord,
Whose manor bounds the utmost planets are.
And clerks and clowns adore, and Thrones and Powers,
Who only see - but we, ah we believe.

    And so exulting with the saints and angels
    We applaud your glory saying

All Holy, holy, holy.....

....

THE INSTITUTION NARRATIVE IN THE NEW TESTAMENT

from The Jerusalem Bible translation

THE INSTITUTION NARRATIVE IN THE NEW TESTAMENT

(from The Jerusalem Bible translation)

In four places the New Testament recounts the institution of the Holy Eucharist. All Eucharistic Prayers synthesize these inspired narratives:

596 Mt. 26:26-29

Now as they were eating,
Jesus took some bread,
and when he had said the
    blessing
he broke it
and gave it to the disciples.
"Take it and eat"; he said
"this is my body."

Then he took a cup,
and when he had returned thanks
he gave it to them.
"Drink all of you from this,"
he said
"for this is my blood,
the blood of the covenant,
which is to be poured out
    for many
for the forgiveness of sins.

From now on, I tell you,
I shall not drink wine
until the day
I drink the new wine with you
in the kingdom of my Father."

597 Mk. 14:22-25

And as they were eating
he took some bread,
and when he had said the
    blessing
he broke it
and gave it to them.
"Take it," he said
"this is my body."

Then he took a cup,
and when he had returned thanks
he gave it to them,
and all drank from it,
and he said to them,
"This is my blood,
the blood of the covenant,
which is to be poured out
    for many.

I tell you solemnly,
I shall not drink any more wine
until the day
I drink the new wine
in the kingdom of God."

598 Lk. 22:19-20, 18

Then he took some bread,

and when he had given thanks,
broke it
and gave it to them,
saying,
"This is my body
which will be given for you;
do this as a memorial of me."

599 1 Cor. 11:23b-26

On the same night that he was
    betrayed,
the Lord Jesus took some bread,
and thanked God for it
and broke it,
and he said,
"This is my body,
which is for you;
do this as a memorial of me."

He did the same with the cup
after supper,
and said,
"This cup is
the new covenant in my blood
which will be poured out
   for you,

...from now on,
I tell you,
I shall not drink wine
until the kingdom of God
   comes."

In the same way
he took the cup after supper,
and said,
"This cup is
the new covenant in my blood
Whenever you drink it,
do this as a memorial of me."

Until the Lord comes,
therefore,
every time you eat this bread
and drink this cup,
you are proclaiming his death.

....

EUCHARISTIC PRAYERS

Note: This is the earliest extant anaphora in all Christian literature, dating from 215 A.D. St. Hippolytus proposed it as a model form, allowing freedom of improvisation to the celebrant. At the time of its writing, the Preface and Sanctus were not parts of the traditional Eucharistic Prayer of the Liturgy. The dialogue adaptation was made by the editor of this book.

PC   Lift up your hearts.
All   We have lifted them up to the Lord.

PC   Let us give thanks to the Lord our God.
All   It is right and just.

PC   We give you thanks, O God,
      through your Son, Jesus Christ,
      whom in this,
      the last of all periods of time,
      you sent to save and redeem us
      and to tell us what you wanted of us.
      He is your Word, inseparable from you.
      You made all things through him
      and you were well pleased with him.

CC   You sent him from heaven to a virgin's womb;
      he lay in that womb and took flesh,
      and you were presented with a Son,
      born of the Holy Spirit and of the virgin.
      He did what you wanted him to do,
      and when he suffered,
      acquiring thereby a holy people for you,
      he stretched out his hands
      to free from suffering
      those who believed in you.

PC,CC When he was handed over
      to undergo the suffering
      he had chosen himself,
      thereby to destroy death,
      to break the chains the devil held us in,
      to crush hell beneath his feet,
      to give light to the just,
      to make a covenant
      and manifest his resurrection,
      he took bread,
      gave thanks, and said to his apostles:
      Take this and eat it,
      this is my Body
      that is to be broken for you.

```
        In the same way
        he took the chalice, saying:
        This is my Blood
        that is to be shed for you.
        When you do this,
        you will be commemorating me.

All     Calling then his death and resurrection to mind,
        we offer you bread and a chalice,
        and we thank you for enabling us
        to stand before you and serve you.

PC      We ask you to send down your Holy Spirit
        on the offering Holy Church makes you,
        to unite all who receive holy communion
        and to fill them with the Holy Spirit,
        for the strengthening of their faith in the truth.

PC,CC   So may we give you praise and glory
        through your Son Jesus Christ.
        Through him may glory and honor be yours,
        Father, Son, and Holy Spirit,
        in holy Church,
        now and throughout all ages.

All     Amen.
```

602 THE EUCHARISTIC PRAYER OF THE ROMAN RITE,
revised by John R. May, S.J.

PC   And now, most merciful Father, we ask you
through Jesus Christ, your Son, our Lord,
to accept and bless (+) these offerings of bread and wine
which we have set apart for your worship
as signs of our gift of self.

We offer this sacrifice to you, first of all,
for the welfare of your Holy Catholic Church,
in union with your servant, _____, our Pope,
and, _____, our Bishop, and all who profess with constancy
the universal faith of the apostles.

Grant to your people, throughout the world,
protection and purpose, peace and unity.

CC   Remember, O Lord, your living servants _____ and _____
      (pause)
and all who have gathered here around your altar.
You know our faith, you have tested our devotion.
Together, we offer to you this sacrifice of praise,
for ourselves and our intentions,
for the atonement of our sins,
and for the personal salvation we hope for. .
To you, eternal God of life and truth,
we address our prayers.

CC   United in the fellowship of your saints,
we venerate their memory,
especially of the glorious, ever-virgin Mary,
mother of our God and Lord, Jesus Christ,
and of blessed Joseph, her spouse.
We recall also your holy apostles and martyrs,
and all your saints.
Through their merits and prayers,
grant us always the help of your strength and protection.

All   This, then, is the offering that we present to you,
we your servants and with us all your people.
Graciously accept it, O Lord;
give us peace all the days of our lives;
and sparing your eternal judgment,
grant that we may be numbered among your elect.

Bless, O Lord, this whole offering
and make it acceptable to you,
perfect and pleasing in your sight--
so that it may become for us
the Body and Blood of your beloved Son,
our Lord Jesus Christ.

PC,CC Who, the night before he died,
        took bread into his holy and venerable hands;
        and raising his eyes in thanksgiving to you, O God,
        his heavenly Father,
        he broke the bread,
        and gave it to his disciples, saying:
        Take this and share it among you,
        for this is my Body.

        In the same manner, after the supper,
        he took this cup of glory into
        his holy and venerable hands,
        he gave thanks again to you,
        and handed the cup to his disciples, with the words:
        Take this and drink from it, all of you:
        for this is the cup of my Blood
        of the new and everlasting Covenant,
        the mystery of fidelity,
        which shall be shed for you and for all men
        to atone for sins.
        Whenever you do this, do it in memory of me.

All   For this very reason, O Lord,
        we your servants and all your holy people,
        remember the blessed passion of Christ our Lord,
        his resurrection from the dead,
        and his ascension into the glory of heaven,
        while we offer, from among your gifts,
        this spotless victim, pure and holy,
        the sacred bread of life everlasting,
        the cup of eternal salvation.

PC   Look with serenity upon these gifts.
        May they please you as did
        the gift of your just servant Abel,
        the offering of our father Abraham,
        and the sacrifice set before you by your priest Melchisedech.
        We humbly ask you, almighty God,
        to bid your holy messenger
        place these gifts in the presence of your divine majesty,
        so that whoever receives from this altar
        your Son's most holy Body and Blood
        may be filled with every grace and blessing of yours.

CC   Remember also, O Lord, your people
        who have gone before us, signed with faith,
        and who sleep in peace, _____ and _____(pause).
        Grant, Lord, to those we have mentioned by name
        and to all who rest in Christ
        a refreshing place of light and peace.

CC   We, your sinful servants, hoping in your boundless mercy,
beg you to grant us the reward and fellowship
of your holy apostles and martyrs,
of John the Baptist and of all the saints.
We pray that we may share their company,
not through any merit of ours,
but because of your loving kindness revealed in Christ.

PC   It is through him that you are continually creating
all the good things that you give to us;
it is through him that you bring them to perfection;
it is through him that you bless them
with the fullness of your Spirit.

All   For through him, and with him, and in him,
all honor and glory is given to you, Father Almighty,
in union with the Holy Spirit,
today and every day until eternity. Amen.

Note: The above prayer, dated July 29, 1967, was composed before
the approval of what has now come to be known as Eucharistic
Prayer I. The above is thus based upon the former Latin
Canon of the Roman Mass.

---

603 EUCHARISTIC PRAYER II

Indeed it is right and fitting,
it is our duty and our salvation
always and everywhere
to give you thanks, (heavenly) Father,
through your beloved Son (OR: only Son), Jesus Christ.
He is the (creative) Word
by which you made the universe.
He is the Savior
you sent to redeem us.
By the power of the Spirit
he was born of a virgin mother.
He opened his arms on the cross
(OR: He opened his hands to the pain of the cross)
to make an end of death
and to show that life would rise again.
Thus did he fulfill your will
and win for you a holy people.
And so we join the angels and the saints
in proclaiming your glory,
all with one voice singing:
HOLY, HOLY, HOLY.....

Lord, you are holy indeed,
the fountain of all holiness.
Send your Spirit to make these offerings holy;
let them become for us
the body and blood of our Lord, Jesus Christ.

Before he was given up to death of his own free will
he took bread and gave you thanks.
He broke the bread,
gave it to his disciples and said:
(OR: Gave it to his disciples and said:)
(OR: and gave it to his disciples, saying:)
Take this and eat,
(for) this is my body
which is given up for you.

So too, after supper, he took the cup,
once more gave you thanks,
and gave the cup to his disciples, saying:
(OR: He gave the cup to his disciples and said:)

Take this, all of you, and drink;
(for) this is the cup of my blood
that ratifies (OR: for) a new and eternal covenant.
It will be shed for you and for all mankind (OR: men)
so that sins may be forgiven.
Do this in memory of me.

Lord, we recall your death,   (Note: to be said
we proclaim your resurrection until you come.   by all(?) - Ed.)

Calling therefore to mind his death and resurrection,
we offer you the bread of life
and the saving cup.
We thank you for holding us worthy
to stand in your presence and serve you.

We also entreat you
that all of us who partake of Christ's body and blood
may be brought together in unity by the Holy Spirit.
(OR: May all of us who partake of Christ's body and blood
      become one by the Holy Spirit.)

Lord, remember and make perfect in love
your Church throughout the world,
especially our Pope, _____,
and our Bishop, _____.

Remember too our friends who have gone to their rest
and hope to rise again.
Remember all the departed
and bring them into the light of your presence.

Show your mercy and love to us all, we pray you.
Make us worthy to share eternal life
with Mary, the (blessed) Mother of God,
with the (holy) apostles,
and with all the saints who have earned your favor.

So may we praise you and give you glory
through your Son, Jesus Christ.
Through him all honor and glory is yours,
with the Holy Spirit in the Church,
now and for ever(more). Amen.

(Rev. 11/29/67)

---

604 EUCHARISTIC PRAYER III
II
Lord, you are holy indeed,
and your entire creation rightly gives you praise.

For all life, all holiness comes from you
by the working of the Holy Spirit
through your Son, Jesus Christ our Lord.
Age after age you form for yourself a people,
so that from east to west
a clean (perfect) offering may be made
to the glory of your name.

III

And so, Lord, we bring you these gifts,
and entreat you to consecrate them by your Spirit.
May they become the body and blood
of your Son, our Lord Jesus Christ,
at whose bidding we celebrate this eucharist (OR: these mysteries).

IV

He, on the night he was betrayed,
took bread and gave you thanks and praise.
He broke the bread and gave it to his disciples, saying:
Take this, all of you, and eat;
(for) this is my body which is to be given up for you.
So, too, after supper, he took the cup
and gave you thanks and praise.
He gave the cup to his disciples, saying:
Take this, all of you and drink;
(for) this is the cup of my blood
that ratifies (OR: for) a new and eternal covenant.
It will be shed for you and for all mankind (OR: men)
so that sins may be forgiven.
Do this in memory of me.

Lord, we recall your death,   (Note: to be said
we proclaim your resurrection until you come.   by all(?) - Ed.)

V

Calling, therefore, to mind the suffering he endured for our
    salvation.
his wonderful resurrection and ascension into heaven,
and proclaiming that he will come a second time,
(OR: So now, Lord, we celebrate the memory
        of the suffering he endured for our salvation.
    We recall his wonderful resurrection and ascension into
        heaven,
    and proclaim that he will come a second time.)
We give you thanks
and offer you this holy and living sacrifice.

VI

We ask you to look with favor on your Church's offering
and accept it as the Victim, the peace-offering of your own choice.
Grant that we, who are nourished on the body and blood of your Son,
may be filled with the Holy Spirit,
and become one body, one spirit in Christ.
May he remake us into an eternal gift to you,
and enable us to win a share in the heritage of your saints,

VII

with Mary, first of all, the blessed Virgin Mother of God;

with your holy apostles and glorious martyrs,
with St. _____, and all your saints.
We rely on their unceasing prayer to help us at your
    judgment-seat.
                    VIII
This offering is to make our peace, Lord, with you.
May it advance the peace and well-being of all the world.
Strengthen in faith and love your pilgrim Church here on earth,
especially your servant, Pope _____, and our Bishop, _____,
with all the bishops of the world
and the entire people your Son has gained for you.
We are the children of your household; grant our prayers.
Father, in mercy and love bring together all your children
wherever they may be.
Welcome into your kingdom our departed friends (brethren)
and all seekers after Christ who have left this world.
We hope to enjoy with them the vision of your glory
for ever and ever.
Through Christ our Lord.
All the good gifts you bestow come to the world through him.
                    IX
Through him,
in him,
with him,
in the unity of the Holy Spirit,
all glory and honor is yours,
almighty Father
for ever and ever.
Amen.

(Rev. 11/29/67)

---

605 EUCHARISTIC PRAYER IV
            I
It is right that we should thank you and glorify you, heavenly
    Father;
you alone are true and living God.
From everlasting to everlasting you live in unapproachable
    (dazzling) light.
Fountain of life, you have created all things;
you have filled your creatures with blessings,
and made many rejoice in the brightness of your light.
Countless hosts of angels, your servants, stand before you.
They look upon the splendor of your countenance,
and glorify you, day and night, unceasingly.
With them we, too, and every creature under heaven,
with one voice praise your name and rejoice, as we sing:
    Holy, holy, holy, Lord God of all might,
    heaven and earth are full of your glory!
    Hosanna in the highest.

Blessed is he who comes in the name of the Lord!
Hosanna in the highest.

II

Heavenly Father, we acknowledge your greatness;
all your works show your (OR: are full of) wisdom and love.
You made man in your own image;
you set him over the whole world;
you made him ruler of every creature so that he might obey you,
    his creator.
Even when he lost your friendship through disobedience
you did not abandon him to the power of death;
you gave help to all that they might seek you and grope after you.
Again and again you made a covenant with men;
through the prophets you taught them to hope for salvation.
Heavenly Father, you loved the world so much
that in the fullness of time (OR: when the fit time came) you sent
    your only Son to be our Savior.
Through the power of the Holy Spirit, he was born of the Virgin
    Mary,
and became man, in all things like us, except that he was without
    sin.
He brought the good news of salvation to the poor,
freedom to prisoners,
joy to those who mourn.
In obedience to your will,
he gave himself up to death;
and then, rising from the dead,
he destroyed death and restored life.
He wished us to live no longer for ourselves but for him, who died
    for us and rose from the dead.
So he sent the Holy Spirit from you, Father,
to complete his work on earth,
and to sanctify every creature.

III

And so, Lord, we ask that this Holy Spirit
(shall) sanctify these offerings
that they may become the Body and Blood of Jesus Christ our Lord
in the celebration of this great mystery
which he left us as an everlasting covenant.
He always loved those who were his own in the world.
When the time came for him to be glorified by you, his heavenly
    Father,
he showed that his love was perfect (OR: showed the depth of his
    love).

While they were at supper,
he took bread, gave you thanks and praise, and broke it.
Then he gave it to his disciples and said:
Take this and eat it.
This is my body which will be given for you.
In the same way, he took the cup,
full of the juice of the vine (OR: full of wine).

He gave you thanks and praise, and gave it to his disciples
    and said:
This is the cup of my blood,
the blood of the new and everlasting covenant,
which is to be shed for you and for all men,
so that sins may be forgiven.
Do this in commemoration of me.

(If the local authority permits, the people may join in the
    prayer with these or similar words:)
Lord, we proclaim your death;
we acknowledge your resurrection till you come again.

                    IV
So now, Lord, we celebrate this memorial of our redemption.
We remember Christ's death (OR: and his descent among the dead):
we proclaim his resurrection and his ascension to your side;
we look forward to his coming in glory.
We offer you his body and blood
as a sacrifice acceptable to you (OR: an acceptable sacrifice)
    which will bring salvation to the whole world.

                    V
Lord, look upon this victim (OR: offering) which you yourself have
    given to your Church;
and to those who shall partake of this bread and wine,
grant in your love that they may be moulded into one body by the
    Holy Spirit,
and so become in Christ a living sacrifice to the praise of your
    glory.

(If the local authority sees fit, the people may join in with
    these or similar words:)
We praise you, we bless you, we glorify you,
Lord, in your love, have mercy on us all.

                    VI
Now, Lord, remember all those for whom we offer this sacrifice.
First, (your servant) _____, our Pope;
_____, our Bishop, and all bishops everywhere.
Remember those who offer this sacrifice, and all here present;
all your people;
all who worship (OR: seek) you with a sincere heart;
and _____ and _____ .

Remember those who had died in the peace of Christ (OR: of your
    Christ, OR: of your anointed Son)
and all the dead whose faith is known to you alone,
and _____, and _____.

Grant also to us, your children,
that we may be made fit to inherit heaven (OR: to receive our
    heavenly inheritance),
with the (blessed) Virgin Mary, the Mother of God,
with your Apostles and saints.

In your kingdom, freed from sin and death,
with every creature, let us sing your glory through Christ
    our Lord,
through whom you give us everything good (OR: all good things).
        VII
Through him,
in him,
with him,
in the unity of the Holy Spirit,
all glory and honor is yours,
almighty Father,
for ever and ever.
Amen.

(Rev. 11/29/67)

_____

606 Joseph A. Appleyard, S.J. (a translation from the Dutch).

PC   The Lord be with you.
All   And with your spirit.

PC   Lift up your hearts.
All   We have lifted them up to the Lord.

PC   Let us give thanks to the Lord our God.
All   It is right and fitting.

PC   We thank you,
Lord, almighty God,
because you are a God of men,
and are not ashamed to be called our God,
because you know us by our names,
because you hold the world in your hands.
For you created us,
and in this life called us to join with you,
to be your people on this earth.
Blessed are you, creator of everything that is,
blessed are you, who have given us freedom
    and life in which to make use of it;
blessed are you in the light we see by,
    in the air that we breathe.
We thank you for the whole of creation,
for all the works that have come from your hands,
for everything that you have done among us,
through Jesus Christ our Lord.
And so, together with every living thing,
we praise your majesty, almighty God.
So do we bow down before you,
and praise you with the words:

All   Holy, Holy, Holy.....

PC   Lord God, our Creator and Father,
how would we ever have learned your Name
if Jesus Christ had not come among us?
For you loved our world so much
that you sent your only-begotten Son
in order that everyone who believes in him
might have life in abundance.
He preached your Name.
He did your will to the very end.
He gave himself to all men.

PC,CC On the night in which he was betrayed
he took bread into his hands,
he raised his eyes to you,
God, his almighty Father.

to his friends

is is my body for you.
inder of me.

the cup,
of thanks said:
ew covenant in my blood
ut for you and for everyone
ss of sins.
rink this cup,
minder of me.   *the Mystery of faith*

at this bread
is cup,
eath of the Lord *Amen*

                                      od,
we perform here this sign of our faith,
and we call to mind
the suffering and death of your Son,
his rising from the dead,
his entrance into your glory,
and that he speaks on our behalf
    from his place at your right hand,
and that he shall come
to judge the living and the dead
on the day that you have determined.

CC   We pray you, Lord God,
All send us your Holy Spirit,
      the Spirit that gives life,
      the power of Jesus Christ.
      We beg you,
      that this bread and this cup,
      our simple offerings,
      may be true signs of our commitment to you,
      that we, together with all the saints,
      may be the Church of Jesus Christ.

All   Through him and with him and in him,
      all glory and honor is yours,
      almighty Father,
      in the oneness of the Holy Spirit,
      for ever and ever.
      Amen.

_____

607   Translated from the Dutch - PREFACE AND SANCTUS, by James
L. Empereur, S.J.; EUCHARISTIC PRAYER, by George Glanzman, S.J., and Frank Ginhac, S.J.

PC   We thank you, Almighty Lord God,
that you are a God of people,
that you are not ashamed to be called our God,
that you know us by our name,
that you keep the world in your hands.
For you have made us and called us in this life
to be united to you, to be your people on this earth.
Blessed are you, maker of all that exists.
Blessed are you, who have given us space and time to live in.
Blessed are you for the light of our eyes
    and the air we breathe.
We thank you for the whole of creation,
for all the works of your hands,
for all you have done in our midst,
through Jesus Christ, our Lord.
Therefore, we praise your majesty, Almighty God,
with all the living;
therefore we bow before you and adore you with the words:

All   Holy, holy, holy, Lord God of all the living.
Earth and heaven are filled with your glory,
We bless your name.
Blessed is he who will come in the midst of his people.
We bless your name.

PC   Blessed are you, almighty God, Father of our Lord Jesus Christ,
blessed are you;
for before the foundation of the world,
you chose us and destined us to be your children.

CC   You have freed us from the power of darkness and brought us
into the light and kingdom of your beloved Son.
He is the image of your glory; for him the universe was made;
in him we have received redemption and forgiveness of sins.

PC,CC On the night on which he was betrayed,
while he was at table with his disciples,
he took bread, said a blessing, broke the bread,
and gave it to them saying;
Take and eat: This is my Body given for you.

Then he took the cup, pronounced the blessing,
and gave it to his disciples, saying:
Drink from this, all of you.
This cup is the New Covenant in my Blood,
poured out for you and for all men
for the forgiveness of sins.
Each time you do this, do it in memory of me.

All   So when we eat this bread and drink from this cup,
we are proclaiming the death of the Lord until he comes.

PC   Therefore, God, our Father, we place here the signs
of our faith,
and we commemorate that he suffered and died,
but most of all that he is the first-born of the dead,
the first-born of the whole creation;
that, glorified at your right hand, he speaks on our behalf.
and we await his coming in glory on the day which
you have appointed.

CC   We pray you, God, our Father, send your Holy Spirit upon us,
the Spirit who brings to life in us the power of Jesus Christ.
We pray that this bread and this cup
which we offer you in humility
may really be the sign of your grace to us.

PC   We pray that, in the midst of this world
and before the eyes of all the people with whom we are united,
we may live your Gospel and be the sign of your peace.
We pray that we may support and serve each other in love;
that our hearts may be open to the poor, the sick, the dying,
and to all who need our aid.

CC   We pray that thus we may be the Church of Jesus Christ,
united with our Bishop _____, and with our Holy Father _____,
and with all believers everywhere on this earth.

PC   Through him and with him and in him
you are blessed and praised, Lord our God, Almighty Father,
with the Holy Spirit,
today and all days until eternity.

All   Amen.

---

608   J. Leo Klein, S.J. (freely adapted from the Dutch).

PC   Our hearts and our voices praise and thank you,
almighty Father,
for you have called all men into being;
your love sustains us all the days of our lives.
     Blessed are you in all the things you have made:
for all the wonders of the world
which are the work of your hands.
     Blessed are you, Father
for giving us eyes to see your goodness
in the things you have made...
ears to hear your word as it calls us...
minds to understand and to love.
     Blessed are you, Father,
for giving us one another as images and reflections
of yourself...
and most of all for giving us your Son, Jesus Christ,
who sums up in himself your love for us
and who alone can show us the way to love in return.
     And so with all of creation and with Christ at our head,
we join in praising and thanking you with these words:

All   Holy, holy, holy.....

PC   Blessed are you, almighty Father,
for before the foundations of the world
you chose us and destined us to become your sons and daughters,
to share your own life with you.
Even when in Adam we had failed to respond in love,
you saved us from our selfishness
and from the power of darkness,
calling us into the kingdom of your beloved Son.
In Christ we are saved and brought back to life with you.

PC,CC   On the night on which he was handed over,
Jesus took bread into his hands;
lifting his eyes to you, his Father, he thanked you.
Then he broke the bread and gave it to his friends
with these words:
Take and eat: This is my body for you.

Then he took the cup,
he said a prayer of thanks over it
and gave it to his friends with these words:
Take this and drink of it.
This is the cup of my blood, of the new and everlasting
covenant...the mystery of faith...
which shall be shed for you and for all others
for the remission of sins.
Each time you drink this cup,
you will do it in memory of me.

All   When we eat of this bread and drink from this cup,
we proclaim the death of the Lord
until that day when he comes again.
And so, Father, we place here this sign of our faith.

CC   We now commemorate and relive Christ's suffering and death,
but most of all we become a part with him
who is the first-born from the dead,
the first-born of the whole creation,
he in whom we are all to find our life.
Glorified now at your right hand,
Christ speaks on our behalf;
he will come to do justice to the living and the dead
on the day you shall appoint.

PC   We pray that this bread and cup which we offer you
in humility in union with Christ
may really be the symbol of our loving surrender to you.
We pray that in the midst of this world,
before the eyes of all the people with whom we are united,
we may live out your gospel and be the continuation
of Christ's love for all men.
May we support and serve each other;
may our hearts be always open to the poor,
the sick, the unwanted,
to all who are in any way in need of our help.
We pray that thus we may truly be the Church of Jesus Christ,
united with our Bishop _____, and our Holy Father _____,
serving one another out of love for you.

CC   We pray, Father,
send your Holy Spirit over these gifts we offer here.
May the presence and the power of the Spirit
bring them to their fullness.
Thus Christ, present in this Bread and Wine
    as our Food and Drink,
will be present in us, and through us
he will be present to the world around us,
where his love desires to transform all creation.

PC,CC It is through Christ,
and with Christ
and in Christ,
that all honor and glory come to you, Father,
in union with the Holy Spirit,
today and all days until the end of time.

All   Amen.

- 51 -

609 EUCHARISTIC PRAYER FOR YOUNG ADULTS, David L. Cooke, S.J.

PC It is most fitting that with our brother Jesus Christ
we thank you for your goodness.
 We thank you, God, creator of the universe
for the air we breathe, the light we sense,
the beauty we see, for the many gifts we share in.
 We thank you, Father, father of Christ and of all men,
for sending us your only-begotten Son
who, in the womb of the Virgin Mary, became man
that he might share in our human condition
and experience our joys and sorrows,
our laughter and pain, our hopes and disappointments.
 We thank you, God our Father,
for the gift of the Word of life
who in our midst grew in wisdom and age and grace,
proclaiming the good news of salvation,
learning and teaching obedience through suffering.
 We thank you for the gift of your Son
who in all things pleased you,
especially by going through death to new life
so as to raise us to the fullness
and freedom of sons of God.
 And so we praise you saying:

All Praised and blessed be God our Father.
For you are all-powerful, all-knowing, all-good.
Praised and blessed be your name,
for you are ever-present, ever-understanding, ever-loving.

PC,CC For this reason, on the night before he died,
he took bread into his hands,
gave thanks to you, God, his Father,
blessed and broke and gave it to his friends saying:
Take this and eat.
This is my body which is being given for you.

In the same way, he took the cup into his hands
and again gave thanks to you,
blessed and gave it to his friends saying:
Take this and drink.
This is the cup of my blood
of the new and eternal covenant,
the mystery of faith,
which shall be shed for you and for all others
unto the remission of sins.

Whenever you eat this bread and drink this cup,
you proclaim this in my name.

PC   Wherefore, Father, we are mindful of the passion,
death, resurrection, and ascension of your Son,
whereby he passed through death to the fullness of life.
    And now together with our risen Lord,
we join ourselves to his perfect act of self-giving.
    As a people made holy by his presence,
we offer to you, Father, this most holy gift,
the perfect and continuing sacrifice of man to God.

All   God our Father, send into our midst your Holy Spirit
so that we may be united in the one body of Christ
through faith, hope, and love.
    In the one Spirit,
may we grow to the fullness of sons and daughters
by serving others and being open to their needs.

CC   May the power of the Spirit abide in the Church,
in _____ our Bishop,
in _____ our Pope, and
in all believers everywhere
so that together we all may praise and bless your name.

PC,CC Through Christ, with Christ, in Christ,
You are praised and blessed,
Lord, Father Almighty,
In the unity of the Holy Spirit,
today and all days until eternity.

All   Amen.

_____

610 CANON FOR YOUNG AMERICANS, James L. Empereur, S.J.

Note: This anaphora is designed for Masses in which all the music is sung in the "folk-tune" style. Its structure is that of a refrain and seven stanzas. The refrain is sung by the congregation; the stanzas are sung by the celebrant. The text of the refrain is taken from the song, "Sons of God," by James Thiem, O.S.B. Although original music may be composed for this canon, it is suggested that the music of James Thiem be used. Both the text of the refrain and the music for both refrain and stanzas are found in Mass for Young Americans by Ray Repp. This canon, then, is sung in the same manner as the song "Sons of God," is sung. There should be guitar accompaniment throughout.

(Refrain):
SONS OF GOD, HEAR HIS HOLY WORD!
GATHER 'ROUND THE TABLE OF THE LORD!
EAT HIS BODY, DRINK HIS BLOOD,
AND WE'LL SING A SONG OF LOVE:
ALLELU, ALLELU, ALLELU, ALLELUIA!

(Stanzas):

1. Glorify the Lord with me;
   Thank Him for the world
      he made;
   Thank Him for our freedom,
   For our life together.
      (Refrain)

2. Thank the Lord for
      He is good;
   Thank Him for this sacred meal
   Which we celebrate today
   As we sing together:
      (Refrain)

3. On the night before He died,
   Jesus blessed and broke
      the bread,
   Saying: Take and eat of this,
   This is my Body.
      (Refrain)

4. Thus He also took the cup,
   Gave it to His friends
      and said:
   This is the chalice of
      my Blood,
   A new pledge never-ending.
      (Refrain)

5. Eat and drink this,
      all of you;
   And you will remember me
   Till I feast again with you
   Where we'll live forever.
      (Refrain)

6. Mindful of our Savior's life
   And His triumph over death,
   Let us offer to our God
   The bread and cup of glory.
      (Refrain)

7. To the Father be all praise;
   Praise to God the Son, our Lord;
   Praise the Spirit in us all;
   Praise our God forever.
      (Refrain)

611 A CANON FOR SMALL CHILDREN, Donald L. Gelpi, S.J.

All   Our Father, we thank you for all the good things
        you give us.
We thank you for our mothers and fathers.
We thank you for our brothers and sisters.
We thank you for our school and for our teachers.
We thank you for watching over us when we play,
        when we study, and when we sleep.
We thank you for making us your children
        and for giving us your Son in this holy communion.

PC   Let us remember now the story of the first communion of Jesus
        with his apostles.
The night before he suffered and died for us,
        Jesus and his apostles had supper together.
And during the supper he told them how much he loved them,
        and how sorry he was that he would have to leave them.
Then, to prove how much he loved them, he took the bread
        that lay on the table. He said a prayer of thanks, broke
        it and gave it to them with these words:
I want you to take this and eat it, for this is my Body.
I am giving it to you.

Then he took a cup of wine and he gave it to them
        with these words:
I want you to take this and drink it.
For this is the cup of my Blood,
the blood of a new and everlasting covenant,
which will be poured out for you and for all men for the
        forgiveness of sins.
Every time you eat this food and drink from this cup,
remember me and how much I have loved you.

All   So we remember that the Lord Jesus loves us more than life.
We remember that he died for us to prove his love.
And we remember that he rose again to give us joy
        and new life.
We ask you to make us happy children, like our brother Jesus.
Please teach us to love one another
        and to be kind to everyone we meet.

PC   For through our brother Jesus Christ, and with him, and in him,
all praise is given to you, God our Father,
together with the Holy Spirit,
forever and ever.

All   Amen.

PC   Lift up your hearts.
All   We lift them up to the Lord.

PC   Let us glorify the Lord.
All   For all his goodness to us.

PC   All glory is yours, Eternal God, who made the universe.
      We praise you for this earth, for life and breath,
      for beauty we have seen and wonders still to come.
      From the beginning, your living Word
      has guided and corrected us.
      Your prophets have called us from disobedience,
      and prepared us for the coming of your Son.

      We praise you for the Christ
      who chose to come as one of us,
      and lived among us full of grace and truth.
      For us he became poor,
      and knew the sadness in our days;
      and for us he died on the cross and was buried.
      In him we know forgiveness and the lifting of burdens.
      He brings light to our darkness
      and opens our eyes to your great glory.

      For you raised him from the dead and set him over all creation.
      Through your Holy Spirit we are members of his body and Church.
      and heirs of the promise of eternal life.
      Therefore we join the faithful
      who, in all times and places, praise your name saying:

All   Holy, holy, holy,
      God of power and majesty,
      heaven and earth are full of your glory.
      O God most high!

PC,CC Holy Father, we thank you that the Lord Jesus,
      on the night when he was arrested, took bread,
      and when he had given thanks, he broke it, and said:
      This is my body
      which is for you.
      Do this in remembering me.

      In the same way,
      he took the cup, after supper, saying:
      This cup is
      the new covenant in my blood.
      Do this, as often as you drink it,
      in remembering me.

CC   We remember you, Lord Jesus, as you commanded,
      confident we shall know you in the breaking of bread.
      We remember you, O Christ,
      confident you will seal the new covenant
      in our hearts as we drink this cup.

PC   O Holy Spirit, who brought us here
      to proclaim the risen Lord,
      unite us in one body with him
      who loved us and gave himself for us.

All   O God, who called us from death to life:
      we give ourselves to you;
      and with the church through all ages,
      we thank you for your saving love
      in Jesus Christ our Lord,
      Amen.

      Our Father.....

_____

613 AN EXPERIMENTAL LITURGY, G. F. Cope, J. G. Davies, D. A. Tytler (dialogue format added and old English pronouns changed to contemporary forms by F. R. Hoey, S.J.).

PC   Lift up your hearts.
All   We lift them up unto the Lord.

PC   Holy are you, eternal Father;
       holy in your redeeming Son;
       holy in your life-giving Spirit.
       Therefore with Angels and Archangels,
       and with all the company of heaven,
       we laud and magnify your glorious Name;
       evermore praising you, and saying,

All   Holy, Holy, Holy, Lord God of hosts,
       heaven and earth are full of your glory.
       Glory be to you, O Lord most High. AMEN.

PC   Let us give thanks unto our Lord God.
All   It is meet and right to do so.

PC   It is very meet,
       right and our bounden duty,
       that we should at all times and in all places
       give thanks unto you,
       O Lord, Holy Father, Almighty, Everlasting God,
       through your beloved Son Jesus Christ,
       by whom you made all things,
       whom you did send in the fullness of time
       to take our nature upon him
       and to suffer death upon the Cross
       for our redemption;

PC,CC Who in the same night that he was betrayed,
       took Bread;
       and when he had given thanks,
       he broke it, and gave it to his disciples, saying,
       Take, eat,
       this is my Body which is given for you:
       Do this in remembrance of me.

       Likewise after supper he took the Cup;
       and, when he had given thanks,
       he gave it to them, saying,
       Drink ye all of this;
       for this is my Blood of the New Covenant,
       which is shed for you and for many
       for the remission of sins:
       Do this, as oft as you shall drink it,
       in remembrance of me.

PC   Therefore, O Father,
      we your humble servants
      recall the blessed passion and death
      of your beloved Son,
      his mighty resurrection
      and glorious ascension,
      until his coming again;
      and we here present unto you,
      through your Holy Spirit,
      this bread of eternal life
      and this cup of everlasting salvation
      that, being made one Body in him,
      we may receive the forgiveness of our sins
      and the joy of your kingdom;

CC   And we beseech you to accept
      this our sacrifice of praise and thanksgiving
      through the mediation of your most dearly beloved Son,
      and so to renew us through your Holy Spirit
      that he may bring forth in us
      the fruits of our redemption,
      and confirm us unto the end;

PC,CC even Jesus Christ your Son our Lord,
      by whom and with whom,
      in the unity of the Holy Spirit,
      all honor and glory be unto you,
      O Father Almighty,
      world without end.

All   Salvation unto God
      who sits upon the throne,
      and unto the Lamb.
      Blessing and glory and wisdom and thanksgiving,
      and honor and power and might
      be unto our God
      for ever and ever. AMEN.

---

614 THE EUCHARISTIC PRAYER OF TAIZÉ (from the Liturgy for Sundays and Festivals, unless otherwise noted).

Preface - (of the Kingdom)

PC   It is truly meet and right, our joy and our salvation,
       to hymn You, bless You, praise You,
       give thanks to You and worship You.
       For You only are God,
       You and Your only-begotten Son, with the Holy Spirit.
       You have brought us into being out of nothing,
       You have raised us when we were fallen;
       You order all things without ceasing,
       that heaven may be open for us,
       and Your Kingdom, which is coming, be granted to us.
       For all Your benefits we give thanks to You,
       and to Your only-begotten Son with the Holy Spirit.
       You whom angels and archangels serve, cherubim and seraphim,
       who sing the hymn of Your victory and proclaim it, saying:

All   Holy, Holy, Holy...

Eucharistic Prayer

PC   Our Father, God of the hosts of heaven,
       fill with Your glory this our sacrifice of praise.
       Bless, perfect and accept this offering as the figure
       of the one and only sacrifice of our Lord.

CC   Send Your Holy Spirit upon us and our Eucharist:
       consecrate this bread to be the Body of Christ
       and this cup to be the Blood of Christ;
       that the Creator Spirit may fulfill
       the word of Your well-beloved Son.

PC,CC Who, in the same night that He was betrayed
       took bread and, when He had given thanks, broke it
       and gave it to His disciples, saying:
       Take, eat, this is My Body which is given for you;
       do this as the memorial of Me.

       Likewise, after supper He took the cup
       and, when He had given thanks,
       He gave it to His disciples, saying:
       Drink you all of this,
       for this cup is the New Covenant in My Blood
       which is shed for you and for many
       for the remission of sins;
       whenever you drink it,
       do this as the memorial of Me.

All   Whenever we eat this Bread and drink this Cup,
we proclaim the Lord's death till He come.

PC   Wherefore, O Lord, we make before You
the memorial of the Incarnation and the Passion of Your Son,
His Resurrection from His sojourn with the dead,
His Ascension into glory in the heavens,
His perpetual intercession for us;
we await and pray for His return.
All things come from You and our only offering
is to recall your gifts and marvelous works.

CC   Moreover, we present to You, O Lord of glory,
as our thanksgiving and intercession
the signs of the eternal sacrifice of Christ,
unique and perfect, living and holy,
the Bread of life which comes down from heaven
and the Cup of the Feast in Your Kingdom.

PC   In Your love and mercy
accept our praise and our prayers in Christ,
as You were pleased to accept
the gifts of Your servant Abel the righteous,
the sacrifices of our Father Abraham,
and of Melchizedek, Your High Priest.

Invocation - (from the Weekday Liturgy)

CC   Grant us the power of the Holy Spirit,
that we may discern the Body and the Blood of Christ...
May this Communion transform our lives,
take away our sins,
fill our hearts with the Holy Spirit,
give us the fullness of the Kingdom of heaven
and confidence before You,
and deliver us from all condemnation,
through Christ our Savior.

PC   By Whom, O Lord,
You do ever create, sanctify, quicken,
bless and give us all Your benefits.

PC,CC By Whom, and with Whom, and in Whom,
be unto You, O Father Almighty,
in the unity of the Holy Spirit,
all honor and glory,
world without end.

All   Amen.

_____

615 CANON FOR THE CHRISTIAN FUNERAL, Rev. Lawrence D. Albertson.

PC   It is fitting indeed and just,
right, and helpful to everlasting life
for us always and everywhere to praise you
and to thank you, Father,
for sending your Son, the Lord Christ Jesus,
who by dying has destroyed our death,
and by rising again has restored us to life.
We are confident and joyful
that life is changed, rather than taken away.
Therefore, with all those who have been summoned
to the fullness of life,
we proclaim your glory again and again
as we join in saying:

All   Holy, holy, holy
Lord God of all things.
Heaven and earth are filled with your glory.
We bless your name.
Holy is he who reveals your presence among us.
We bless your name.

PC   Most loving Father,
through the sending of your Son, the Lord Christ Jesus,
you have given us the way to peace, joy,
and love of everlasting life.
Mindful of the promise of Christ:
"He who eats my flesh and drinks my blood
has life everlasting
and I will raise him up on the last day,"
we ask you to recall your great deeds of love
which brought new life to those who loved you.
We are thankful for the breath of life which you have given us.
We are thankful for the promise of new life
made to Abraham, Isaac, and Jacob
which you fulfilled in bringing forth
your beloved and chosen people
from a life of slavery in Egypt
to the new life of freedom and joy in the promised land.

CC   Now we thank you for the sending of your beloved one
who has made us one in your love.
We ask you to bless these gifts of food and drink,
which we have offered to you,
that they may become the bread of life
and the drink of love and joy
which your Son, our Lord Christ Jesus,
has promised to those who share them.

PC,CC On the night before he suffered,
he took bread into his hands,
and lifting his eyes to you, the beloved Father,
he gave thanks, and breaking the bread,
gave it to his brethren, saying:
Take and eat this bread;
For this is my body,
which is being given for you.

Then he took the cup,
and again giving thanks to you, the beloved Father,
he gave the cup to his brethren, saying:
Take the cup, and drink this wine;
For this is the cup of my blood
which is being shed for you and for many.
Do this in memory of me.

PC In loving memory of the Lord Christ Jesus,
we offer you, most loving Father,
the bread of eternal life
and the wine of unending joy,
recalling to mind the passion of your suffering servant,
the resurrection and ascension of the Lord Jesus,
and the coming of the Spirit of love and truth
who leads us to you, the eternal Father.

CC May this Spirit of love and truth come to us
through this bread of everlasting life
and in this cup of unending joy
and lead us back to you, Our Father.
We ask you to be mindful of the breath of life
which your Son brought to the son of the widow of Naim,
and especially to Lazarus,
whom the Lord Jesus loved and restored to life.

PC,CC We offer this memorial of love,
to you, the Father of us all,
that through the Lord Jesus,
with the Lord Jesus,
and in the Lord Jesus,
all honor and all glory
be given to you through the power of the Spirit,
forever and ever and ever.

All Amen.

————————————————

616 Robert W. Cavanagh, S.J.

PC   We give You Thanks, O Lord, for showing Yourself to be,
in every way, the God of Love, our Father.
For, in Your mysterious love,
You chose to create, to share Your eternal goodness.
You had need of nothing, yet You made the universe --
so vast, beautiful, and complex --
for us, the people You made in Your own image.
And when we turned away from You, Lord,
and began to live for ourselves instead of for You,
You were merciful: You worked for our salvation.
You intervened in history and over the centuries
revealed Yourself and Your saving plan to the people of Israel.
But this, the old covenant,
was just the foreshadowing of what was to come --
the mystery that had been kept hidden through eternal ages.

CC   Moved by the intense love You had for us --
even though we were dead because of our sins --
You made us live with the life of Christ, Your own Son,
who, though He is by nature God,
did not consider this a condition to be clung to, but,
when the fullness of time came, He emptied Himself
by taking on our mortal nature and humbled Himself so that
He might experience the agony of death
for the sake of every human being.

CC   For in Him it pleased You, Father, to reconcile everyone
to Yourself and to make peace both on earth and in heaven
through the blood shed on the cross.

PC   Together with Christ Jesus and in Him, you raised us up
and enthroned us in the heavenly realm, sending down upon us
the Spirit of adoption and giving us the power to become
children of God and heirs of life everlasting.

All   So, Father, in order that we may unite ourselves
with Your Son and participate with Him
in the saving mysteries of His death and resurrection,
we have gathered together to eat the Lord's Supper,
in which He again makes present for us those saving deeds.

PC,CC   For on the night He was betrayed,
Jesus took bread into His hands;
and, after giving thanks,
He broke it and gave it to His friends
with these words:
Take this, all of you, and eat.
For this is my Body
which will be given for you.

In the same way, after He had finished the supper,
He took the chalice in His hands
and said:
Take this, all of you, and drink.
For this is the chalice of my Blood
of the new and everlasting covenant,
the mystery of faith,
which will be shed for you and for many others
for the forgiveness of sins.
As often as you do this,
you will do it as my memorial.

All   And so, Father, every time we eat this bread
and drink the chalice of the Lord,
we proclaim His death until He comes.

CC   And in response to the great love You first showed us,
we dedicate ourselves to follow Christ
by dying to sin and selfishness
and by living out the two great commandments which he gave us:
to love You, Father, above all things and to love one another.

PC   And, guided in our task by the Holy Spirit
living in the Church,
we offer our entire lives for the spreading of the Gospel
among men of every class and nation,
until the designated time,
when all men will enjoy the freedom of the children of God
and You gather all creation under one head,
Jesus Christ, our Lord.

All   For it is through Him and with Him and in Him
that all honor and glory are given to You,
God, Almighty Father,
in union with the Holy Spirit,
now and for all eternity.
Amen.

---

617 CANON OF CHRISTIAN SERVICE, by Clyde Crews.

PC   We praise you, O God, because of your own free gift of love
        you have reached out to man
        and with the patience of a Father wait for him
        to break the chains of selfishness
        and to respond to your love in kind.
We lift up our hearts
        and acknowledge you as the God who is with us always,
        closer to us than we are to ourselves.
You have made us, Father. You know us.
You stand by us both in suffering and in joy.
We honor your creation all about us.
For you we seek to fill our minds with everything that is true,
        everything that is noble, everything that is good and pure,
        everything that we love and honor, and
        everything that can be thought virtuous or worthy of praise.
Thus we know that you are the God of Peace
        and you are truly with us.
For this reason we make our own the words
        which your prophet Isaiah spoke for your people Israel:

All   Holy, holy, holy.....

PC   We gather together now to celebrate that One who comes,
        Christ Jesus, who graciously makes himself present
        in our midst through the power of the Holy Spirit.

In union with your whole church, with our Pope _____, and
        our Bishop _____, we come to proclaim the faith and hope
        we place in you, O God.
We come to make manifest the love we have for one another,
        both those who return our love and those who do not.
We pray that the life of your Son Jesus may lead us
        to be more sensitive to all who need our aid:
        the poor, the lonely, the sick;
        the wicked as well as the good.
And we pray that we may be quick to see our own needs
        and humble enough to ask the aid of our brothers.

CC   You have indeed constituted us as brothers, O God,
all   through your Son,
        in order to share a common task in the world
        and a common joy and union with you
        in the time which you have appointed.
You have exhorted us to fill the earth,
        to subdue it and re-consecrate it to you.
We pledge ourselves to the task in all its pains
        and exaltations;
        for we can persevere only if we know
        that you are both our guide and our goal.

PC We know that you have called us to this common destiny
        and do in fact stand with us,
        for you have sent your Son, Jesus,
        who became man and shared our life
        so that we may share his divine life with you.
    May we ever keep in mind the way he lived and died among us --
        for he emptied himself and took the form of a servant,
        faithful in his obedience even unto death.

PC,CC It was as a servant that he appeared to share
    his final meal with his friends.
    For he took the bread that lay before him;
    he praised you, his Almighty Father, broke the bread,
    and gave it to his friends, saying:
    Take this. Eat it. For this is my Body.
    It is given for you.

    He also took a cup and passed it among them, saying:
    Take this and drink. This is the cup of my Blood,
    of the new and everlasting Covenant, the mystery of faith,
    which shall be shed for you and for all others
    unto the remission of sins.
    Whenever you do these things, you will commemorate me.

Let Us Proclaim the Mystery of faith

All It is this memory and this present reality before us
        that unites us in this ~~victory~~ celebration.
    For his death was revealed as victory by his resurrection
            in power.
    And in his victory is our triumph,
        for he has become our high priest and is ever able
        to save us who draw near to you through him,
        since he always lives to make intercession for us.

PC For we have not a high priest
        who is unable to sympathize with our weaknesses,
        but one who in every respect has been tempted as we are,
            yet without sinning.

All *PC.* For through him and with him and in him,
    all honor and glory is yours, O God our Father,
    in the unity of the Holy Spirit,
    today and all days until eternity. Amen.

        (The Lord's Prayer)

PC Because Jesus, our brother, now reigns in majesty,
        we can make bold to call upon you, O God,
        with the name of Father,
        and pray as your Son taught us,
        saying:

All   Our Father in heaven,
        may your name be held holy, may your kingdom come,
        may your will be done, on earth as in heaven.
    Give us today the bread we need.
    Forgive us our faults
        as we forgive those who have wronged us.
    And do not put us to the test but save us from Evil.

PC   Save us, merciful Father, for we know that we are in quest
        and struggle until we rest in you.
    We labor to change the world
        with the love with which you have graced us.
    But our sins are many. We now freely confess to you, Father,
        and to one another the selfish weaknesses
        that keep us from doing your will.
    May then, the receiving of the Body and Blood of your Son
        be a present remedy and the pledge of future glory.
    We ask this through Christ our Lord.

All   Amen.

        (Prayers Before Communion)

PC   In eating this Body and drinking this Blood
        we proclaim the death of the Lord until he comes again;
        for he is coming to approve and complete our efforts and
        our growth, to root out iniquity and to make all things new.
    And the kingdom of the world will be the kingdom of our God
        and of his Christ.

    Confident in this promise of the Lord,
        let us reach out now to one another
        in a new dedication of our lives to
            the One who is in us all.
            (The Kiss of Peace is given; then PC continues:)
    As the power of the Lord our God has changed
        the bread and the wine,
            those products of our human industry,
        so may all of us be nourished and transformed
        as we set out again on our work in the world.
    For the world belongs to us. And we are Christ's.
    And Christ is God's.

All   Amen. Come, Lord Jesus.

_____

618 CANON OF DEATH AND RESURRECTION, Francis Dowling, S.J.; as revised by James K. Serrick, S.J.

PC   We come together to thank you, Lord God,
to thank you especially in Christ Jesus, your dear Son.
You called him and you sent him to us.
And he answered your call so freely, so totally,
that we are still overwhelmed at this example;
and we still walk in the bright light
he brought into this world, his world and ours.
We thank you for him,
especially that he was so much at home here with us,
and that, like us, he too longed for a love imperishable,
for a life unending.
As friend and brother,
he shared all our joys, all our sorrows;
yet he ever remained your true Son, faithful and obedient.
We thank you and adore you, Father, especially for him,
who did all the great human things --
    like being born of a woman,
    like eating and drinking with friends,
    yes, like dying --
as with full heart
he gave himself completely to this world.

PC,CC For that is just what he was doing
on the night he was delivered up.
He took the bread, said the blessing, broke the bread,
and gave it to his disciples saying:
Take this, all of you, and eat it:
This is my body which will be given up for you.

In the same way, he took the cup, filled with wine.
He gave you thanks, and giving the cup to his disciples,
    said:
Take this, all of you, and drink from it:
This is the cup of my blood,
the blood of the new and everlasting covenant.
It will be shed for you and for all men,
so that sins may be forgiven.
Do this in memory of me.

PC   Let us proclaim the mystery of faith.

All   Christ has died. Christ is risen. Christ will come again.

PC,CC That is why, Lord God, we are offering
this sign of our faith,
and that is why we now recall his sufferings,
    his crucifixion,
    his death,
    his burial.

Yet above all, we joyfully recall
    how you brought him back to life,
    how you brought him back to us,
    how you exalted his name above every other name,
    him, that unforgettable man who lived with us,
    who prayed for us,
    who will come again to make all things new.
Then, no one will sorrow,
no one will die;
He will call each of us -- that great Son of yours,
each of us by our own name
on that day you have already picked out.

CC   So we ask you, Lord God,
to send us his total power and love,
your Holy Spirit,
so that, full of hope,
we can get on with our tasks on earth, arm in arm,
all the while taking care
that no one of your people walks alone.
We pray that we may be peacemakers,
and be happy,
and that we may find you, and close by you,
all that have gone before us.
We pray that we may see you, and talk with you, Father,
as one friend to another, in the presence of Jesus, your Son,
through whom you give us everything that is good.

PC,CC Through him, with him, in him,
in the unity of the Holy Spirit,
all glory and honr is yours, Almighty Father,
forever and ever.

All   Amen.

---

619   THE CANON OF CHRISTIAN HOPE, Ernest C. Ferlita, S.J.

PC   We thank you, Almighty God,
Father of our Lord Jesus Christ
because in him you have fulfilled every promise,
in him you have anchored every hope.
He has himself become our hope,
because you raised him from the dead
and gave him glory.
In this spirit of thanksgiving,
we bless your name;
and with all your creation
we lift our voices in a hymn of praise, saying:

All   Holy, holy, holy.....

PC   We hope in you, Almighty God,
because from the very beginning
you gave us your word of promise.
Even when we turned away from you in sin,
breaking the covenant we made with you,
you did not forget us
but called us back to your table.
I will give them a New Law, you said,
and I will write it upon their hearts.
I will be their God,
and they shall be my people.

CC   And so, in your own good time,
you sent us your only Son.
Born of Mary,
he became as we are,
and he carried in his heart
all our hopes and expectations.
He said to us, If anyone is hungry,
let him come to me.
And again, If anyone is thirsty,
I will refresh him.

PC,CC   Then, on the night before he died,
he gathered his friends together for a final meal.
Recalling your great mercy, Almighty Father,
he took bread into his hands,
broke it, and said:
Take this, and eat it, all of you;
This is my Body.

When supper was ended,
he took the cup,
and when he had given thanks,
he gave it to his disciples, and said:

Take this, and drink from it, all of you;
This is the cup of my Blood,
The Blood of the new and everlasting covenant --
the Mystery of Faith.
This Blood is to be shed for you and for all men,
so that sins may be forgiven.
Whenever you do this,
you will do it in memory of me.

PC   So now, ~~Lord~~ *Father*, with hope in our hearts,
we celebrate the memory of Christ, your Son.
We, your people and your ministers,
recall how he suffered and died for us,
with your name upon his lips.
He trusted in you,
and you raised him from the dead,
receiving him into your glory.

CC   To this glory we look forward,
and our hope is not deceptive,
because you have given us your Spirit
as the seal of your everlasting love.
Urged by this same Holy Spirit,
we offer you these gifts of your own making,
the living bread,
and the saving cup.
By eating of the one bread,
and drinking from the same cup,
we profess our union with you and with one another,
in the one Church of Jesus Christ.

All   *Father,* Open our minds to the future, ~~Lord,~~
~~and do not let us despair.~~
Open your hearts to whomever we meet on the way,
and bring us, with all your creation,
to the perfect fulfillment of our hopes,
in Christ Jesus our Lord.

PC,CC   Through him, in him, with him,
in the unity of the Holy Spirit,
all glory and honor is yours, almighty Father,
forever and ever.

All   Amen.

- 72 -

PC   To you, Almighty Father, we give thanks and praise.
For it was you that made the heavens,
the sun and the moon and the stars.
It was you that established the earth,
you that gave breath to its people
     To this people you said,
I did not make the earth to lie idle,
I made it to be your home.
And so they drew from it bread and wine,
and opened rivers in the rock.
They raised up cities from the ground,
and sang new songs in the air.
     So now, with all your creation,
we give you thanks and praise,
through your Son Jesus Christ our Lord.
He is before all things,
and he holds all things in unity.
He was there when the morning stars sang together,
and all the angels shouted for joy.
Now we join our voices to theirs, saying:

All   Holy, holy, holy.....

PC   We thank you, Almighty Father,
for sending him to dwell among us,
born of the people of Abraham
whom you multiplied as the stars of heaven,
and the sands of the seashore;
born of the people of Moses
whom you led through the desert,
going before them in a pillar of fire and cloud;
born of the daughter of Sion,
in whom the promise of his coming was fulfilled
and the sign of our fulfillment given.

CC   We thank you for the good news that he proclaimed
and for all that he did in our midst.
He fed the hungry,
and said that his food was to do your will.
He gave drink to the thirsty,
and taught us to thirst for the living water.
He healed the sick,
and declared his power to forgive sins.
He let his glance fall on the lonely,
and showed us that God is love.

PC,CC Above all, we thank you for the love he bore us
     till the end.
Knowing that you had put everything into his hands,
that he had come from you

and that he was going back to you,
he took his place at table,
and his apostles with him, and said,
I have longed to eat this passover with you
before I suffer;
I tell you, I shall not eat it again
until it is fulfilled in the kingdom of God.
And then he took bread,
and gave thanks to you, his Almighty Father.
He broke the bread
and gave it to those whom he loved, saying:
Take this, all of you, and eat.
This is my Body,
which is to be given for you.

In the same way, he took the cup,
and when he had given thanks,
he shared it with all who were gathered there, saying:
Take this and drink.
This is the cup of my Blood,
the blood of the new and everlasting covenant.
This blood shall be poured out for you and for all,
for the forgiveness of sins.
Whenever you do these things,
you shall do them in memory of me.

PC   Still in pilgrimage upon this earth,
we trace in trial and under oppression the paths he trod,
remembering how he suffered and died for us,
and rose on the third day, just as he had said,
the firstborn from the dead.
We do not lose heart,
for we trust that he will come again in all his glory
to restore and establish those who believe in him.

CC   And so we offer you, most merciful Father,
through your beloved Son,
this sacrifice of praise and thanksgiving,
in union with _____, our Pope, with _____, our Bishop,
and with all your people.
May it be a sign of our communion
in the one perfect sacrifice of your Son.
For we know that we come from you,
and that with him we shall go back to you.

All   Send down upon us all, therefore, your Holy Spirit,
that he may make of us yet more perfectly
    a royal priesthood
empowered to proclaim before all men your saving name
and to speak their names in your presence;
that he may make of us yet more truly a people

striving toward that Day when you shall be all in all,
everything to everyone,
the Day of our Lord and Savior Jesus Christ your Son.

PC,CC Through him, and with him, and in him,
You are blessed and praised, Almighty God our Father,
in the unity of the Holy Spirit,
now and forever.

All   Amen.

June 2, 1967;
revised:
September 1, 1968

621 PRAYER OF THANKSGIVING, Peter E. Fink, S.J.

PC   Father, we give you thanks always and everywhere
for the great blessings we have received
from your hands.
By the power of your touch you gave us life
and raised us to a dignity
far beyond all that we deserve.
We alone, of all your creation,
can call you Father,
and offer you praise that is pleasing to you.
We join now in prayer
about the table of your Son
and offer you thanks at his request.
Hear us, Father,
as we join our voices to all you have made
and proclaim this hymn of praise
to your holy name:

All   Holy, Holy, Holy...

PC   We give you thanks, Father, and we sing your praise
for all the wonderful works you have done in our midst.
You led our fathers, the children of Israel,
from the land of Egypt
and set them free from the bonds of slavery
which held them captive.

CC   You gave us, in the slaughter of the lamb,
that first Passover
to be a sign of our own deliverance from sin.
Through Moses you made a covenant with your people
by which you bound yourself to us in love forever.

CC   You showed us your regard for loving trust in you
by your generous fulfillment of the promises
you made to Abraham.
Little by little, and in many different ways,
you made yourself known to us by the prophets;
and finally, in the fullness of time,
you spoke to us in a Son.

PC   This Son came to us in mystery,
as a sign of contradiction to this world.
By his life, he showed us how to live;
by his love, he showed us how to love.
He did not want to leave us, but wished to stay with us
even after his mission on earth was accomplished.
On the day before he suffered and died for us
he left us a sign
in which he would always be among us and for us.

PC,CC   While he was together with his friends at dinner,
        he took bread into his hands.
        He raised his eyes to you, Father, and gave you thanks.
        He blessed the bread and gave it to his friends,
        saying:
        Take and eat of this, all of you:
        This is my Body which is given for you.

        In the same way, as the dinner came to an end,
        he took a cup of wine.
        Once more he gave thanks to you, Father;
        he blessed the cup and passed it to his friends,
        saying:
        Taking this cup and drink from it:
        This is the cup of my Blood, the sign of the new and
        lasting covenant which my Father now makes with you.
        This Blood shall be shed for you and for many
        so that sins may be forgiven.
        Do this in memory of me.

All   Heavenly Father, we give you thanks for the gift
        you have given us in Christ Jesus your Son.
        We recall his life, death, and victorious resurrection,
        and we proclaim our faith in his presence among us.

PC   Send your Spirit upon us, and these our gifts.
        Grant that through them we may do honor to you
        and be worthy to be called your sons.

CC   Holy Father, keep us all by your power.
        Make us one with each other and with you
        just as you are one
        with the Holy Spirit and with your Son.
        We do not ask you to take us from the world,
        but only to keep us from harm.
        You sent your Son into this world;
        so he has sent us that the world might believe.
        It is not for us alone that we make this request,
        but for all who come to believe in you
        through our word.
        Let us all be one in you that the world may believe
        that you sent us.

PC   We pray again the prayer of your Son, Jesus Christ,
        and ask its fulfillment in his name.
        It is ever through him that all good gifts are created
        by you, given life, and bestowed upon us.

All   Through him, with him, and in him,
        we give you honor and glory,
        together with the Holy Spirit,
        forever and ever. Amen.

(The Lord's Prayer)

PC   Let us pray:
We express now our common bond of brotherhood
by praying in the words our Lord has given us to pray:

All   Our Father.....

PC   To you, Father, who by the power at work within us,
are able to do far more abundantly than all that
we ask or think,
to you be glory in the Church and in Christ Jesus
to all generations, for ever and ever.

All   Amen.

(At the Communion)

All   As often as we eat of this Bread and drink from this Cup,
we proclaim the life, death, and resurrection of the Lord,
until he comes again.

(After Communion)

PC   There is only one Body, one Spirit, one faith,
which your Son Jesus Christ has called us to share.
Because Christ has promised that our union with one another
here on earth will lead to everlasting union with you,
help us overcome all barriers
and be drawn ever closer to each other and to all men.
We ask this in the name of Christ.

All   Amen.

(Dismissal and Blessing)

PC   May the Lord bless you and keep you.
May he make his face shine upon you.
May the Lord look kindly upon you
    and give you his peace.
And may Almighty God bless you,
Father, Son, and Holy Spirit.

All   Amen.

PC   Let us go now in peace.

All   Thanks be to God.

---

622   CANON OF THE BREAD OF LIFE, Donald L. Gelpi, S.J.

PC   Truly holy and truly blessed are you, Father of life;
for in your wisdom and fidelity you long ago freed
your chosen people from the bonds of their oppressors,
and by your law, you taught them to live as free men
in the fertile land which you had promised to their fathers.

By the hand of Moses you led them through the desert;
you guided them tenderly as a shepherd leads his flock,
you sheltered them as a hen shelters her chicks
     beneath her wing.
Yet they murmured against you in their pride; and though
they had seen your power in their passage through the waters,
yet in their hunger and thirst they forgot your saving mercy.
They tested you in the desert and questioned the fidelity
     of your covenant.

CC   But boundless is your kindness, Almighty Father;
for though your anger blazed at their ingratitude,
you remembered that they were only creatures made of flesh;
and with a father's care you spread for them a banquet
     in the wilderness.
You gave them the food of angels, the bread from heaven
which contains every delight and which satisfies every hunger.
To quench their thirst, you opened the rock,
and made living waters flow from it as a promise and a portent
     of everlasting life.

PC   For all these things you did only as a figure of the final act
of grace which you have accomplished now in the mission
     of your Son.
He is the true rock from which flow the living waters;
he is our passage from slavery to freedom,
your everlasting covenant of hope
which you have concluded with your faithful children.
He is the true bread which comes down from heaven
in order to give life to the world.

All   Whoever comes to him will never hunger,
whoever believes in him will never thirst, and
whoever comes he will not turn away.
By faith in him we are sustained in our trial.
By belief in his word we are daily nourished.
By the power of his grace we are strengthened
     in our pilgrimage.
For whoever eats the flesh of the Lord and drinks his blood,
lives in the Lord, just as the Lord lives in him.

CC   For the flesh of the Lord is real food,
and his blood is real drink,
and his words are the message of eternal life.

For you have sent your Son into our midst
as one who draws his life from you,
and you have promised that the man who shall receive him
in this sacred banquet of renewal,
shall draw his life from the Lord.
This, then, is the bread come down from heaven,
not like the bread our forefathers ate -- for they are dead.
Whoever eats this bread will live forever.

(PC pauses for a moment of recollection.)

PC   And so we recall now
       that the Lord Jesus on the evening he was betrayed
       gathered together his disciples for a final meal.
       He comforted them in their sorrow and dismay,
       called them his friends, and bade them place in him
       the same confidence which we owe to you, Father of Life.
       For as he took leave of them, he assured them that
       he would return again after preparing for them and for all
       who would believe in him an everlasting dwelling
           in his Father's home.

PC,CC Then he took the bread which lay before them,
       he thanked you, Father, for your kindness.
       And he broke the bread and gave it to them
           with the words:
       Take this. Eat it. For this is my Body.
       It is being broken for you. Do this in memory of me.

       And in the same way he took the cup and gave it to them
           with the words:
       Take this. Share it among you.
       For this is the cup of my Blood,
       the blood of a new and everlasting covenant,
       the mystery of fidelity
       which will be shed for you and for all men
       for the forgiveness of sins.
       Do this also in memory of me.

All   Drawn, then, by living faith, we offer you ourselves
       in union with your Son,
       who is present in these consecrated signs of our salvation;
       and we recall with thankful hearts that the Lord Jesus
       suffered and died for us and rose again in glory
       so that by his death we might learn to die to our
           selfishness and weakness.

PC   For we have believed the message which he taught us:
       Unless a grain of wheat falls into the ground and dies,
       it remains only a single grain;
       but if it dies, it yields an abundant harvest.
       And therefore we remember that though he died,

Yet in your fidelity you have raised him from the dead,
    Father of Life,
and that you have appointed the day when those who sleep
in death will, like Lazarus, abandon their graves at the
    sound of his voice.
For you have entrusted all judgment to him,
so that on the last day he may give life to those
whom he has chosen as his friends.

CC   Renew in us, then, we beg you, O God,
the gift of his life-giving Spirit,
who alone can quench our thirst for fulfillment
with an abundance of living water.
Confirm us in your grace as we share together this food
    from heaven,
transform us into new bread, holy and unleavened,
and grant that this sacrificial banquet may truly be for us
a renewal of our love for one another
and of our fidelity to him who is our Food and our Life.

All   For through him, and with him, and in him,
you are blessed and praised, God our Father,
in the unity of the Holy Spirit,
today and all days,
until eternity:
Amen.

---

623 CANON OF THE LIGHT OF GOD, Donald L. Gelpi, S.J.

PC   Truly holy are you and truly blessed, Father of Light,
for you have rescued your people and have gathered together
the scattered remnant of your flock.
In a pillar of fire, you have led us from the place
     of our bondage;
from the valley of darkness, from the farthest horizons,
you have gathered us together to rejoice and find contentment
     in your presence.
For nothing is impossible to you, O God; and yet
in your compassion you have concluded with us an everlasting
     covenant of love and hope.

all
cc *   Holy and blessed are you in your Son, Jesus Christ our Lord,
who has risen in glory upon our world of sadness and shadows.
He is our everlasting covenant of grace,
the true Light who enlightens every man who comes
     into this world.
Whoever believes in him need never remain in darkness,
but advances always to the light of a new dawn.
For whoever looks to him with the eyes of faith, looks upon
     your saving power, most merciful Father.

All   For you have so loved the world that you have given us
your only Son in order that everyone who believes in him
may never perish, but may find in him everlasting life.
You did not send him to condemn the world, but in order that
the world might be enlightened and saved through him.
For the man who believes in him is not condemned;
but the man who does not believe has already been condemned,
for refusing to believe in the glory of God's only Son.

cc
all   And the judgment is this:
that the Light has come into the world, but men preferred
darkness to light, because their deeds were evil.
For whoever practices the works of wickedness hates the light,
and shuns it lest his deeds be exposed.
But whoever lives in the truth comes into the Light,
so that the Light may manifest that his deeds are done in God.

PC   Enlightened, then, and comforted by your gracious kindness,
     God our Father,
we call to mind that on the evening of his final passover,
even as the powers of darkness gathered their forces about him,
the Lord Jesus gathered together his twelve apostles,
to initiate with them a new and everlasting covenant of grace.
And we recall that though he was their Lord and Master,
he rose from table, girded himself like a slave,
     and washed their feet,
in order to teach them the extent of his love and of the love
they should bear one another in his name.

PC,CC Then, in order to make of them a new Israel,
       he took the bread which lay before them,
       he praised you, Father in heaven, for your faithfulness.
       Then he broke the bread and gave it to them
           with the words:
       Take this. Eat it. For this is my Body.
       It is being given for you.
       Do this in memory of me.

       And in the same way he took the cup and gave it to them
           with the words:
       Take this. Share it among you.
       For this is the cup of my Blood,
       the blood of a new and everlasting covenant,
       the mystery of fidelity,
       which will be shed for you and for all men
       for the forgiveness of sins.
       Do this also in memory of me.

PC   Conscious, then, of the light of your grace, we offer you,
       in union with your Son, these consecrated signs of his death
       and exaltation and of his saving presence in our midst.
       Accept them, we pray, as a pledge of our fidelity and
       of our unshaken hope in the glory of his second coming.
       For we believe that he shall appear again like the brightness
           of the sun
       and shall scatter forever the clouds and the darkness;
       and the glory of his countenance shall light up all creation.

All   Until the dawning of that day,
       strengthen and enlighten us, we beseech you, O God,
       by the abundant Wisdom of your Holy Spirit.
       Guide us along the paths we must follow;
       and so strengthen and unite us that we may by the power
       of your grace truly become a light among the nations.
       So may we truly become your people
       and the Church of Jesus Christ.

PC,CC For through him, and with him, and in him,
       you are blessed and praised, God our Father,
       in the unity of the Holy Spirit,
       today and all days,
       until eternity.

All   Amen.

---

624 CANON OF THE WORD OF GOD, Donald L. Gelpi, S.J.

PC   We praise you and we bless you, eternal Father,
that in the fullness of time you have spoken to us
your saving words of graciousness and of love.
For by the message of your Son, you have called us
to be your children and your friends.
And by the light of your word we are warmed and strengthened
    in our darkness and loneliness.

CC   We bless the power of your creative word,
which first drew out from the waters of chaos
the rich, firm land where we now live and work,
the word that sustains the heavens and the stars,
and the measureless immensity of space.

All   We bless the kindness of your words of forgiveness and of
promise that you spoke to our first parents in their shame.

CC   We bless your word of hope that long ago summoned Abraham
from the darkness and ignorance of unbelief
and called him to be our true father in the faith.

All   We bless your summoning word that raised up Moses and
the prophets to bear witness against the infidelity and
injustice of mankind, and to cleave our hearts with
the two-edged sword of righteousness and of truth.

PC   But most of all we bless you for your Son.
For he is your first and final Word of love,
the all-encompassing Wisdom who proceeds from your lips,
the Alpha and the Omega, the Beginning and the End.
By him we are created anew.
In him we find redemption and forgiveness of sins.
Through him we are summoned to confess the power of your love
and are sent forth to proclaim the good news of our salvation
    in humility and in truth.
With him we die and are born to a new life.

PC,CC We recall the immensity of his love for us, which led him
to stretch out his arms to embrace the cross,
that your fidelity to him and to a sinful world
    might be revealed.
For the night before he suffered, with great longing,
he gathered together his friends for a final meal;
and knowing full well all that was still to come,
    he looked upon them with love.
Then he took the bread that lay before them;
he praised you his eternal Father, for your faithfulness;
he broke the bread and gave it to his friends saying:
Take this. Eat it. For this is my Body.
It is being given for you.

And in the same way he took the cup and gave it to them
   with the words:
Take this. Share it among you.
For this is the cup of my Blood,
the blood of a new and everlasting covenant,
the mystery of fidelity,
which will be shed for you and for all men
for the forgiveness of sins.
As for you, when you do these things, do them in memory
   of me.

All   We recall these words in gratitude and love;
and in obedience we ponder this mystery of the lifting up
of your Son, our Lord Jesus Christ,
in hope and expectation of the great day
when he shall appear again before the eyes of all men
       in majesty and in might.
And in the everlasting power of his command, we offer you
this sign of our belief and of his saving presence
       in our midst.

PC   We ask you to renew in us now the Spirit of your Son,
that we may learn from him and from his memory the true
meaning of love and that we may find in him an unquenchable
       thirst for justice and for peace.

CC   We pray for one another and we ask you to bless us.
Be favorable to our Pope _____ and to our Bishop _____,
and to all the pastors of your Church throughout the world.
Preserve in them a concern for the unity of your flock,
that they may guide it in meekness and in truth.
Grant to us, your people, the courage to live our lives
       in the image of your Son.

PC   Increase in us a concern for those whom you love,
for the lonely, for the poor, for the homeless,
for the defenseless, that we may labor in your name
to restore to them their rightful dignity as your adopted
       sons and daughters.
Please bless our President and our land, and keep us blameless
       in your sight.
So, our Father, may you always be pleased with us, even as
you were ever pleased to look upon the face of your Son
and servant, our Lord, Jesus Christ.

All   For through him, and with him, and in him,
you are blessed and praised, God our Father,
in the unity of the Holy Spirit,
today and all days until eternity.
Amen.

625 Benedict J. Habiger, O.S.B.

Note: Space limitations require some editing of Fr. Habiger's introductory explanation to this Eucharistic Prayer, and do not permit including the detailed and scholarly footnotes with which he documented every statement.

The simple consecratory act of Christ at the Last Supper was gradually enveloped by a ritual of prayer and ceremony. The purpose of these elaborations was to explain the mystery of the Eucharist and to give it a certain amount of dignity.

Due to abuses during the period of "charismatic improvisation" there began a movement to organize the various anaphoras into a standard formula. The high point of this evolution seems to have come in the sixth century during the reign of Gregory the Great. According to liturgists, the words and actions of this liturgy were not only very meaningful in themselves, but they were natural and intelligible to the people who participated in the liturgy of the Eucharist. Gradually, due to many factors through the centuries, communication between priest and people lessened to the point where the Mass eventually became the private affair of the celebrant. The liturgy, then, in many instances became a dead letter.

The liturgy of the Mass, with its readings, offertory, canon and communion, is basically the same today as it was in the sixth century. In modern times a great deal of stress is rightly being given to the priesthood of the laity. In order to promote greater participation of the faithful in the renewal of the Eucharistic mystery, the prayers of the faithful have been restored, and the offertory procession has again found a place in our liturgy.

Although the vernacular has been allowed for the canon of the Mass, it still contains a number of serious difficulties. Besides the fact that it is a sixth century formulation, it has acquired a number of accretions through the centuries that have disrupted its original continuity. A prime example is the Memento of the Dead including the Nobis quoque.

Today, particularly in view of Vatican II, Christian spiritual life has a slightly different orientation. There will always be a real need for personal prayer, penance, and sacrifices. But instead of being oriented to the individual self, they are being more directed toward the service of society. The stress is upon mutual assistance among men in the Spirit of Christ for the building up of God's creation.

Besides the many new developments in society today, there are also a good many significant developments taking place in the field of theology as a result of modern thought and scholarship.

If these developments are true and reasonable, then there is no reason why the best part of them should not be identified in some manner with the renewing of Christ's sacramental presence among his people. Such an approach gives greater realization to a deeper understanding of the future eschatological fulfillment of all things in Christ.

The purpose of the Constitution on the Sacred Liturgy is four-fold, as stated in its introduction:
"This sacred Council has several aims in view: it desires to impart an ever increasing vigor to the Christian life of the faithful; to adapt more suitably to the needs of our own times those institutions which are subject to change, to foster whatever can promote union among all who believe in Christ, to strengthen whatever can help to call the whole of mankind into the household of the Church. The council therefore sees particularly cogent reasons for undertaking the reform and promotion of the liturgy."
In view of these objectives of Vatican II the following anaphora is an attempt to make use of recent developments in theology in order to give greater meaning to the liturgical celebration of the Eucharist in modern times.

As Christ came to win the hearts of men to God, not their sacrifices, a conscious effort has been made to avoid the offering of gifts for their own sake, a concept which can easily be mistaken from a number of texts in the offertory and canon prayers.

In view of the great work done by Scheeben on The Mysteries of Christianity, and of later theologians concerning our relationship to the Trinity, the following anaphora is an effort to enable the faithful to identify themselves with God's redemptive activity. The procedure by which this is accomplished begins with a recognition of our present situation. The theme of salvation history is taken up and developed through the anaphora. Within this context the main events of God's self-revelation are renewed. Instead of the one "great Amen" at the end of the present anaphora, an effort has been made to give God's people an opportunity to respond more intelligently to his saving acts. This is done by a short prayer, said by the people and addressed to each of the divine persons at specific points in the anaphora.

The prayers in preparation for communion following the traditional canon have been dropped, and the time for communion moved into the anaphora itself. As suggested by the synoptic accounts, communion time is located after the words of consecration.

The intercession of the Saints and a prayer for the Poor Souls are taken up towards the end of the anaphora. Before closing, there is a prayer for unity followed by a petition of the faithful for a blessing before returning to their various walks of life. The Eucharistic celebration is completed with the blessing.

Although this anaphora does attempt to give greater meaning to the celebration of the Eucharist, it makes no effort to solve the problems which it may create. It is merely an attempt to give greater clarity to the central mystery of our Faith.

It may be argued that the length of this anaphoa does not render it practical for use. In answer to this objection it is suggested that, since the main doctrines contained in the <u>Gloria</u> and <u>Credo</u> are dealt with in the anaphora within the context of salvation history, the repetition of these credal formulas becomes repetitious in the liturgy of the word. It has been suggested that on weekdays, however, a shortened form of some anaphora be used, which may highlight some particular aspect of the Eucharistic mystery.

ANAPHORA

<u>PC</u>   May the Lord bless us.
<u>All</u> And renew his presence among us.
<u>PC</u>   Let us lift up our hearts to the Lord.
<u>All</u> That they may be filled with his divine life.

(<u>Address to the Father</u>)

<u>PC</u>   O God, having come together from our various walks of life,
we wish to praise you for this magnificent world of creation
in which you have placed us.
To each one of us you have given the precious gift of life.
You have given us the power to observe the order,
beauty, and grandeur of your handiwork.
You provide us with the air we breathe
and the food we eat.
Unable to fully understand all that you have done,
we marvel at them,
praise you for your magnificent work of creation,
and pray that we may be able to help
bring all these things to their ultimate perfection
in you, O God, our heavenly Father,
through Christ our Lord.

<u>All</u> Heavenly Father, the God of creation,
heaven and earth are filled with your glory.
Holy and blessed are you who have done such wonders.
May we be worthy and effective ministers
in this earthly kingdom of yours.

<u>PC</u>   Almighty Father, we your people have not always been faithful
to you,
for we have broken the laws of nature and done harm to each
other.
In your great mercy you saw the chaos into which we had
plunged ourselves,
and you reached out to help us.

CC   To show us the right way, you selected Israel
       and promised your assistance to these people.
       But, like ourselves, they often ignored your offer.
       You continually raised up prophets among them
       to reprimand and direct them along the right path.
       You even gave them a king to rule in your name.
       Still, your people continued to fall back into their erring
            ways.
       A few there were, however, who remained faithful to you
       even through suffering and persecution.
       To these, O Holy Father, you promised a Messiah
       who would bring them a new life filled with happiness.

                    (Address to the Son)
PC   Exceeding all expectations, you sent your own Son to help us.
       As God, and as man born of the Blessed Virgin Mary,
       Jesus Christ our Lord marvelously assumed our fallen nature
       and elevated it into the light of your divine life,
       O Holy Father.

CC   In perfect fulfillment of his Father's will,
       our Lord Jesus Christ did not fear to die upon the Cross
       in order to break the bonds of our sins,
       so that we might be free to enter into the divine life
       which he came to bring.

PC,CC O Lord Jesus Christ, on the night
       before you allowed yourself to be sacrificed for
            our sake,
       you took bread into your hands and gave thanks.
       Then, having lifted up your eyes to your heavenly Father,
       you broke the bread and gave it to your disciples
       with the words:
       Take and eat, this is my Body.

       You also took a cup of wine,
       and offering a prayer of thanks over it,
       handed it to your disciples
       saying:
       This is the cup of my Blood
       of the New Covenant,
       which shall be shed for all men
       unto the remission of sin.

All   Holy, holy, holy,
       we praise you Lord Jesus Christ,
       Son of the eternal Father.
       We adore and thank you for having come
       to bring us your divine life.
       May this new life which we have received in Baptism
       now be nourished by the Body and Blood
       of your own glorified body.

(Here, all partake of the Body and Blood of Christ.)

PC   Lord Jesus Christ, Son of the Eternal Father,
in order that you might continue to dwell with your people
in a most intimate manner,
you have given us your glorified body
to eat and drink in the form of bread and wine.
We thank you for having given to your Apostles and their
    successors
the power of repeating your action of consecration.
Mindful of your great love and of your complete gift
of self to us on the Cross,
we offer you in return, O Lord Jesus Christ,
our entire lives with all that we do and have.

CC   By your Resurrection you not only destroyed the threat
    of death,
but you showed us the way into a new and everlasting reality.
Having ascended to heaven,
you are seated at the right hand of the eternal Father
from which you will one day come to judge
the living and the dead.

At Pentecost you sent forth your Spirit upon the disciples,
which even now is continuously being poured out upon us
through the sacraments,
animating our frail natures with your divine life
according to our various needs in life.

(Address to the Holy Spirit)

PC   O Holy Spirit, the eternal bond of love
between the Father and the Son,
open our ears to the saving Word of God
and drop the scales of bias from our eyes
that we may be able to see the needs
of God's developing kingdom around us.
Free us from the bonds of our own self-centeredness,
that we may have an open heart to be of service to our
    fellow men.
Refresh our entire being with your divine love.
Strengthen us with the fire of divine love to face our own
    limitations
and to meet the difficulties and dangers of life.
Open our fearful hearts to the needs of the poor,
the sick, the suffering and dying,
so that we may be able to support and serve the needs
of each other in love.

All   O Holy Spirit, the new and everlasting life
which Christ has poured out upon us from the Cross,
help us to return Christ's love by laying down our lives
for him in the service of our fellow men.

Pour your gifts into this community,
that being strengthened by one another
we may grow to greater unity
in your divine love, O Holy Spirit.

(Address to the Saints)

PC In order that each of us may be faithful
to the gifts we have received from God,
and be able to give ourselves with greater dedication
to our duties and the needs of others,
we beg the intercession of all who have found
their eternal happiness in God.
May those Saints whose patronage we were given at Baptism
help us to reach our full maturity in God's life.

- Pause -

(Plea for Poor Souls)

CC On behalf of all those who have departed from this life
and have not yet attained their fulfillment in your divine life
O Lord God, we beg you to consider our sacrifices
and the afflictions we endure,
and grant to those suffering souls
the eternal rest which their hearts desire.

- Pause -

(Prayer for Unity)

PC Fellow Christians, let us never forget
that Christ has risen from the dead.
Having received his Spirit,
whereby we have become the adopted children of God,
let us unite ourselves visibly to Christ.
May our unity with his visible representative on earth,
Pope _____, and our Bishop _____,
enable us to work efficiently
as members of one Ecclesial body
in the service of our fellow men
for the greater honor and glory of God.

All Almighty Father, eternal Son, and Holy Spirit,
be with us as we return to our various walks of life.
Help us to build up your kingdom on earth
in a way that will profit us for all eternity.

(Concluding Blessing)

PC May the blessing of the Father, Son, and Holy Spirit
be always with you. Go in peace.

All Amen.

626 VALYERMO CANON, J. J. Kaufmann, as revised by
R. F. Hoey, S.J.

PC   Our thanks to you, Father, for your Son, our Lord and Brother,
Jesus Christ, whom you sent to redeem us.
For he is Emmanuel, the Messiah,
whose forerunner was John the Baptist.

CC   He came to us through the Virgin Mary, who, by the power
of the Holy Spirit, became the Mother of God
and is the mother of us all.

PC,CC   Before Christ our Brother went to the Cross,
he met for the Passover Meal with the Apostles,
the meal he had looked forward to so longingly.
He took bread, blessed it, broke it, and gave it to them,
   saying:
Take this and eat it. For it is now my Body.

When the meal was finished, he took the cup, blessed it,
and gave it to them saying:
Take this cup and drink from it;
this wine is now my Blood,
to be shed for the remission of sins.
Do this in memory of me.

All   We call upon the Holy Spirit to empower us, Father,
to take these gifts here before us, the Body and Blood
of your Son, and be filled with the supremacy of love
as he was and is.

PC   We pray now for our Holy Father, Pope N., our Bishop, N.,
and for all the shepherds of your people.
May their example of love and service inspire all men
of good will to share in the Eucharistic Meal that is the
sign of the eternal Covenant between you, Father, and
   the People of God.

CC   Remember, Father, those who have gone before us.
Remember also those of us still on earth as members of
the Pilgrim Church, especially N.,
that the greatest of all gifts of the Spirit,
the charism of love may be manifest to all here and now.

PC   Through Christ, and with Christ, and in Christ,
all honor and glory is given to you,
eternal Father,
in union with the Holy Spirit,
now and all days.

All   Amen.

627

Anne C. Kenney

PC   From time out of mind, Father,
You have loved us.
You brought us into Your world
to do Your work and to live Your love.
You keep us alive and well
so that we may live with and for You.
You send us trials and pain
to teach us the paradox of Love --
the mystery of living You.
And so, Father,
we come together today as a community
to praise and thank You,
to express our sorrow and to ask Your guidance,
as we share our love with our brothers.

CC   We remember Your many acts of love
towards us and the peoples of all time.
We thank You for all those we love
whom You have given to us.
We ask You to keep them safe
and to bless them forever.
We pray also for ourselves --
that we may continue to grow in Your love
and may always have the courage
to live the faith we believe.

All   We remember today, as we gather
around Your altar in peace,
the night on which Jesus,
Your Son and our Brother,
gave to His disciples the gift
of His Body and His Blood.
This is a gift for all peoples --
in all times and all places --
a gift of His love.

PC,CC   He took the bread and blessed it.
Then He broke it and gave it to each of them
in love, with the words:
Take this and eat it,
all of you:
This is My Body for you.

Then He took the cup, and
after blessing it, gave it to each of them
and said:
Drink of this, all of you:
For this is the cup of My Blood,
which I will shed for you and for all men
so that your sins may be forgiven.

All   Each time we eat of this Bread
        and drink from this Cup,
        we do it in memory of Him.

PC   We thank You, Father,
        for the gift of Your Son.
        As He loved each person He met
        while living among us,
        help us to love each one we meet
        along our road to You.

CC   As we stand before You today
        committed to You and living in joy,
        we pray for peace in the world --
        peace among all peoples,
        and especially peace for each man
        within himself.

CC   We realize, Father, that without You
        we can do nothing.
        Humbly placing our trust in You
        we renew our dedication to You
        who are as real to us
        as we are to each other.

All   We ask you to send upon us
        the Spirit of Love,
        so that we may be able to continue
        Your work of creation
        in the little circle that we call our world.
        We are far from perfect, Father,
        but with the Spirit of Love
        we can learn to live the life
        that we are called to live.

PC   We adore You now through Jesus Christ,
        Your Son and our Brother,
        who died an ignominious death
        that with Him we might live forever.

All   Through Him,
        with Him, and
        in Him,
        all honor and glory are Yours,
        Father Almighty,
        in the unity of the Holy Spirit,
        who moves us in infinite ways,
        forever and ever.
        Amen.

628

from THE MASS REFORMED, by Roger Kuhn, pp. 73-74.

PC   The Lord be with you.
All And with you also.

PC   Lift up your hearts!
All We hold them up to the Lord!

PC   Let us give thanks to our Lord God!
All That is our privilege and duty!

PC   It certainly is our privilege and duty,
our right and salvation
to give you thanks always and everywhere,
Lord, holy Father, almighty and eternal God...
...And so, with the angels and archangels and with
the whole company of heaven, we sing unending praise
to your glory:

All Holy, holy, holy is the Lord, the God of hosts!
The heavens and the earth are filled with your glory!
Hosanna in the heavens!
Blessings on him who comes in the name of the Lord!
Hosanna in the heavens!

PC   As the glory and credit belong to you, almighty God our Father,
it is to you that we offer, bind, and commit ourselves
now with these gifts,
in thanks for giving your Son to become one of us
and to suffer death upon the cross for our salvation,
showing there by his obedience the way to your forgiveness.

CC   And as he set up, and commanded us to continue, this banquet
in memory of his sacrifice until he comes back,
we pray you to bless with your Holy Spirit these our gifts,
your creatures of bread and wine,
that they may become for us the body and blood of your Son:
welcome offerings in your sight
and nourishing to our salvation.

PC,CC For your Son our Lord Jesus Christ on the night
of his arrest
took bread and, after giving thanks to you,
broke it and gave it to his disciples with the words:
"Take this and eat; this is my body, given for you."

Then he took a cup, and having offered thanks to you,
he gave it to them with the words:
"Drink from it, all of you; for this is my blood,
the blood of the new covenant, shed for you and for many
for the forgiveness of sins.
Do this in memory of me."

PC   So, loving Father, Lord of heaven and earth,
we your servants together with all your holy Church
do celebrate before you the banquet he has commanded,
offering up to you that sacrifice without defect:
the bread of eternal life and the cup of everlasting salvation,
in memory of your Son's obedience in dying
and of your mercy in raising him back to life
and taking him to live forever with you.

CC   Looking for his coming again with glory,
we ask you mercifully to accept this our sacrifice
of praise and thanksgiving.
Together with the service of our whole life,
begging you to forgive our sins,
to raise us also back to life
and take us to live forever with you.

PC   We pray you to fill us now with the power of your Holy Spirit
so that all we who share in the sacrifice of your Son
by tasting these offerings of his body and blood
may more and more be made one body with him,
living always in him and he in us
for the sake of building your kingdom here.

PC,CC And therefore as these and all your blessings
come down through your Son
to us in the fellowship of your Holy Spirit,
all the credit, all our praise and dedication
we give you, God our loving Father,
in fellowship with your Spirit
and through your Son,
our Brother and Spokesman: Jesus Christ the Lord,
now and forever!

All   Amen.

———————————————————

629   John C. L'Heureux, S.J.

PC   We give you praise and thanks, Almighty Father,
          that you are God, creator and Father of all men.
      You know us and so we live.
      You love us and so we are your people.
      Blessed are you, Father, that you have given us
          this day and this hour.
      Blessed are you, Father, in all the things you have made:
          in plants and in animals and in men,
          the wonders of your hand.
      Blessed are you, Father, for the food we eat;
          for bread and for wine and for laughter in your presence.
      Blessed are you, Father, that you have given us
          eyes to see your goodness in the things you have made,
          ears to hear your word,
          hands that we may touch and bless and understand.
      We give you thanks that, having made all things, you keep
          them and love them. And so with all your creation, we
          praise you through our Lord Jesus Christ, saying:

All   Holy, holy, holy, Lord God of all things,
      Heaven and earth are filled with your glory.
      We bless your name.
      Holy is he who reveals your presence among us.
      We bless your name.

PC   We offer you, most merciful Father, through your Son
          Jesus Christ, this sacrifice of praise.
      You have chosen us to be your children,
          you have called us to a life of joy and love
          by giving us your beloved Son.
      We wish to offer you ourselves in this,
          your Son's most holy sacrifice.
      We pray for the welfare of your Church,
          for our Bishop _____, for our Pope _____, for all believers,
          and for all unbelievers everywhere.

CC   We remember with love the Blessed Virgin Mary,
          Mother of our Lord Jesus Christ;
          we remember his holy apostles, his martyrs, and his saints.
      We ask for peace everywhere on earth, peace among all men
          who still do not know that we are brothers.
      We ask that, loving one another in the bonds of peace,
          we may love you as your Son has loved you.
      Through him we praise you, Father, through your Son
          Jesus Christ.
      He has revealed your love to us.
      He is the image and the incarnation of your presence.
      He has become man for us.

PC Though he is the first-born of all creation,
   you sent him from heaven to a virgin's womb.
 He took flesh and was born of the virgin
   and of the Holy Spirit.
 He did all things that were pleasing to you:
   he grew and he obeyed and he loved you
   even to his death for us on the cross.

PC,CC Before he was handed over to undergo the suffering
 he accepted for us,
 thereby to free us from death and selfishness and sin,
 to bring light to a darkened world,
 to make a new covenant of love and mercy,
 he took bread into his hands, gave thanks, broke it,
 and gave it to his friends, saying:
 Take this and eat.
 This is my Body which is to be broken for you.

 In the same way, he took the cup, gave thanks,
 and gave it to his friends, saying:
 Take this and drink.
 This is my Blood
 which is to be shed for you and for all others
 the cup of the new and everlasting covenant
 for the forgiveness of sins and the promise
 of life forever.
 Whenever you do these things, you will be
 commemorating me.

All As often as we eat of this bread and drink of this cup,
 we proclaim the death of the Lord until he comes.

   (Those attending the Mass may wish to recite the
    remainder of the Canon along with the Celebrant.)

PC And so, Lord God, we commemorate now that he suffered
 and died for us, that he has triumphed over death
 and lives forever glorious in his resurrection,
 that he sits at your right hand and speaks on our behalf, and
 that he will come to judge the living and the dead on the day
   you shall appoint.

CC We pray that this perfect sacrifice of your Son
 which we offer you in humility and love
 may be the sign of our surrender to you.
 We pray that before the eyes of all men
 we may live your Gospel and witness to Christ's presence,
 that we may support one another in love,
 that our hearts may be open to the poor, the sick,
 the unwanted, to all who are in need.
 We pray that thus we may truly be the Church of Jesus Christ,
 serving one another out of love for you.

PC   And so, Lord God, we eat of this body and drink of this blood
       of your Son Jesus Christ
       as the sign of our faith
       and as the food of our life in Christ.

All   Through him and with him and in him
       you are blessed and praised,
       Almighty God our Father,
       together with the Holy Spirit,
       now and forever.
       Amen.

            (The Lord's Prayer may be recited while communion is
             distributed, and the Gloria when the last of the wine
             has been consumed.)

_____

630 EUCHARISTIC PRAYER OF HUMAN UNITY, John R. May, S.J.

PC   We thank you, Almighty God, Father of all men,
for sharing with us the love that makes you one
with your Son and with the Holy Spirit.
We praise you and thank you for calling us through faith
to share your gift of love with the world
and so to hasten the fulfillment of your promise to reunite
the world and all men in your Son, Christ Jesus, our Lord.
With loving gratitude, we bless your name; and joining
in the chorus of creation, we celebrate your presence
with this hymn of praise:

All: Holy, holy, holy...

PC   Blessed are you, gracious Father, for from the beginning,
you made us masters of the earth and brothers to all men,
born in your likeness and sharing a common destiny.
It was our pride, though, that made us deaf to your voice
and blinded us to the beauty of your plan.
For you created us to fill the earth and have dominion over
it, but, of our own perversity, we preferred to be ruled
by the world and to wear the mark of Cain.
You created us to live in harmony with our fellow men,
but we preferred alienation and the Babel of many tongues.
You created us to welcome your approach in the quiet
    of evening,
but we preferred to know our nakedness and to hide
    from your love.

CC   Nonetheless, in your loving kindness,
you did not allow our house to remain divided against itself.
For you made alliances with Abraham and Moses and David,
preparing the people for the coming of One
who would crush the head of division and pride,
who would gather together again the broken fragments of Adam
throughout the world, and forge them into a new and
    far greater unity than we had ever known.
Thus, in the fullness of time, you sent your only Son
into the world to call by name into one fold
the scattered children of your flock,
to make of those who believe in him the living stones of
    your only Temple,
to mold the diverse gifts of your people into the members
    of one Body, which is his Church.

PC,CC For on the night before he died,
he called together his friends for a final meal,
and made with them a new and everlasting covenant
    of love,
by sharing with them his own body and blood.

Giving thanks to you, almighty Father,
he took bread into his hands, broke it and said:
Take this and share it among you,
for this is my Body, which is for you.
Do this as a memorial of me.

Then he took a cup of wine,
and offering thanks to you again,
gave it to them with the words:
Drink from this, all of you, for this is my Blood,
the cup of the new covenant, the mystery of fidelity,
poured out for you for the forgiveness of sins.
Whenever you drink of this, do it as a memorial of me.

CC   And so, in loving response to his command,
we recall that he was obedient unto death,
even to death upon a cross,
but that you raised him up from the dead
and gave him a name that is above all names,
so that all men together might acknowledge him as Lord;
and, through him, you poured out your Spirit upon his apostles
to restore to mankind the unity that had been lost through sin,
fusing the parted tongues of Babel into the flames
    of a single fire.
Placing here, then, this sign of his sacrifice,
we unite ourselves to him, who gave his life
that we may be one, even as you and he are one.

All   Merciful Father, we beg you to send the Holy Spirit among us
in a new Pentecost of understanding and harmony,
so that whoever speaks the truth in love
will be heard by each man in his own tongue.
For in sharing one bread and drinking from the same cup,
we profess our faith in the power of the Spirit
to bend our pride into love and our selfishness into unity.

PC   Grant us concern for our fellow men,
even for those whom we have never seen or called by name.
May we suffer with the victims of hatred and oppression,
of starvation and war.
Grant us a selfless love for each other, so that our unity
may be the genuine sign that it claims to be,
heralding that final and blessed union of all men
in Christ Jesus our Lord.

All   For through him, and with him, and in him,
all honor and glory is given to you, almighty Father,
in union with the Holy Spirit,
today and every day until eternity.
Amen.

---

631 CANON OF THE LOVE OF GOD, Elisabeth A. Meier.

PC   Blessed are you, O God, Father of our Lord Jesus Christ,
for you have blessed us with all the spiritual blessings
    of heaven in him.
Before the world was made, you chose us to be holy and
    blameless before you.
You destined us in love to be your sons in Christ Jesus,
to make us praise the glory of your grace,
your free gift to us in him by whose blood
we gained our freedom and the forgiveness of sins.
Therefore, with all creation let our voices join
in praise and love for you, our Father, as we say:

All   Holy, holy, holy...

PC   We give you thanks, Father, that you have loved us so much
that you sent your own Son to be our brother,
so that everyone who opens his heart to him
may find life in you.
We know that you have loved each one of us
from the beginning of time when you created the earth,
and men to walk upon it, and blessed them.
In your great care for us you chose for yourself a people,
you brought them out of bondage and gave them all good things.
And when they, too, were unfaithful to you,
you sent your prophets to call them back to your way.
When they still did not respond to this call,
you surpassed yourself in love
by giving us your only Son to die for us.

CC   Therefore, we pray for the Church which we love
and through which you manifest your presence to us.
Bless our Pope, _____, and our Bishop, _____,
and all your priests and people.
Grant peace and unity to all men who serve you.
United with one another in your Son
we ask you, Father, to send your Spirit upon us.
Give us the strength to live your love every day of our lives.
Bless and accept these gifts of bread and wine and of
ourselves which we offer to you now.

PC,CC In this spirit, then, let us recall the supper
    of the Lord.
For on the day on which he was betrayed,
the Lord Jesus, in his great love for us, took bread;
giving thanks, he broke it,
and gave it to his disciples, saying:
Take this and eat. This is my Body, which is to be
    broken for you.

In the same manner, after supper, he took the cup,
blessed it, and gave it to those whom he loved, saying:
Take this and drink.
This cup is the new covenant in my Blood,
the mystery of faith,
which will be poured out for you and for all men
for the forgiveness of sins.
Whenever you do these things, do them in memory of me.

All So when we eat this bread and drink from this cup,
we proclaim the love of Christ until he comes.

PC Holy Father, we your children, together with your whole Church,
celebrate here before you the sacrifice of your Son,
calling to mind his great love and obedience to you,
 even to death,
your mercy in raising him to life,
and his presence in our midst now and forever.
We offer you this act of praise and thanksgiving
and the service of our lives
in love and gratitude for your great gifts to us.

CC We pray that we may love one another as you love us.
For we believe that all love comes from you
and that everyone who loves is begotten by you
and abides in you and in your Son.
For you live in us and your love is brought to perfection
 in us.
May we share this your gift of love
by giving of ourselves to all your creatures,
even to those who do not love us in return.
For we know that in love there can be no fear,
and that fear is driven out by your love.

PC We believe that nothing on this earth
can ever separate us from your great love for us
in Christ Jesus our Lord.

All Therefore, in joy and confidence, we offer you, Father,
the body and blood of your Son.
For through him and with him and in him,
all honor and glory is yours,
in the unity of the Holy Spirit,
today and all days, until eternity.
Amen.

PC   We give you thanks, Holy Father,
and we proclaim your love in our midst.
You are our Lord who has called us into life in your image.
When in Adam we tasted the bitter fruits of sin and death,
you, ever faithful, did not leave us in our despair.

All   We give you thanks, God of Israel,
who promised to Abraham, our father in the faith,
a chosen people to be a light among the nations.
When we were in slavery, you raised up Moses
     to break our chains.
You united us in the first paschal meal.
You led us through the sea toward the land of freedom.
You joined us to yourself in the alliance of mercy.
You raised your tent among us in the desert,
     and dwelt in our sanctuary in Jerusalem.
When we abandoned you unfaithfully, you sent your prophets
     to summon us to your love once more.

CC   We give you thanks, eternal Father; in the fullness of time
you sent your Son to become our Brother.
Born of Mary, he lived our life, growing in wisdom,
     stature, and grace.
He was announced by John the Baptist;
he walked among us and announced your presence
     in his word and work.
But his own received him not.
When his hour had come, in loving obedience to you
     and fidelity to us,
he submitted to the power of death, the just for the unjust.
And because he laid down his life for his brothers,
you raised him up in glory and made him Lord and Savior,
     the new man of all men.

PC,CC We give you thanks, Father of Love,
who has given us the pentecostal spirit of your Son.
You gathered us here to be the beginning
     of a new creation.
Through you we pass from slavery to freedom,
     from egotism to brotherhood.

In this spirit we recall the supper of the Lord.
The day before he suffered
he took bread into his holy and venerable hands
and lifting his eyes heavenward to you,
God, his all-powerful Father,
gave you thanks by pronouncing the blessing.
He broke the bread and gave it to his disciples, saying:
All of you, take and eat this, for this is my body.

Likewise, after the supper
he also took this glorious cup into his holy and
    venerable hands.
He gave thanks to you by pronouncing the blessing
and gave it to his disciples, saying:
All of you, take and drink from this,
for this is the cup of my blood,
the blood of the new and eternal covenant,
the sacrament proclaiming our faith,
to be poured out for you and all men,
to obtain the forgiveness of sins.
Whenever you perform these actions,
    do them as a memorial of me.

All   We recall in gratitude this great mystery of our salvation;
the death, resurrection, and ascension of your Son,
    Jesus Christ our Lord.

CC   We offer you this sacrifice:
pure, holy, and immaculate,
the sacred bread of eternal life, the chalice of salvation.
Father, together with Christ our Brother,
we offer you the bread and wine of our lives,
in home, in work, in community.

PC   We pray you, holy Father,
that your Spirit may protect us from sin and maintain us
    in unity.
May this holy meal lead to our perfect family banquet
in the New Creation, through Christ our Lord.

All   Through him,
and with him,
and in him.
Amen.

(This Eucharistic Prayer comes from the parish of San Miguelito in
the outskirts of Panama City, Panama, where it is apparently being
used on an experimental basis.)

_____

- 105 -

633 EUCHARISTIC PRAYER FROM "THE CANA-FEAST LITURGY,"
Joseph A. Tetlow, S.J. (composed for a wedding ceremony).

PC The Lord be with you.
All And may he give you his Spirit.

PC Lift up your hearts.
All Our hearts are already with the Lord.

PC We owe thanks to the Lord.
All Yes, it is only right to thank him.

PC This is why it is right, almighty Master, for us to thank you:
that you brought from nothing
a universe of beauty and splendor,
from darkness you brought light,
and from chaos, order and growth
under your own providence.
    We thank you that you crowned this earth with human kind.
And we must thank you that you are our God
and have patiently taught us
to call you our maker, our Lord, our Father.
    For though each of us is born of man and woman,
it is to you that we owe thanks
for the joy of living and being,
for our breath and light, our place and times,
for making us the selves that we are
among the other selves you surround us with.
    This is why we join ourselves
with all the minds and voices who know you and praise you
and raise our hearts and tongues in this angelic song:

All Holy, holy, holy, Lord God of hosts!
Heaven and earth are filled with your glory.
Hosanna in the highest.

PC We thank you, God of light and wisdom,
that your joy was to be in person among the children of men.
For when the appointed time came,
you sent your only-begotten Son among us,
born of woman like each of us though you alone are his Father,
to work our redemption.

All He it is who revealed to us that you have loved us first,
and all we owe you in return is love.
He it is, your Word and Wisdom, who made known to us
the Personal community of love
among Father, and Son, and Spirit.

CC Therefore he taught us,
whom you made in your image and likeness,
a new command, which brings us more and more

into the image and likeness of your own being.
He taught us that love is above all creative;
he taught us how we are to share the divine life of love
and that if we love as you have loved,
we have fulfilled all the Law
and become members one of another in his own Mystical Body.
   Therefore we raise our voices
with deep thankfulness and praise him who comes:

All   Blessed is he who comes in the Name of the Lord.
      Hosanna in the highest.

PC   Finally, your well-loved Son gave the greatest sign of love
      by laying down his life for the redemption
      of those his Father had given him.
         Now therefore we remember the command
      he gave us on the night before he died.
         Joined with the whole Church,
      with our Sovereign Pontiff _____,
      with _____, who is our shepherd,
      and with all of your faithful people.
         Remembering your holy Mother Mary,
      remembering the apostles with whom
      you first shared your Flesh and Blood,
      and remembering the martyrs and all the saints.

All   We your faithful people ask that this sacrifice
      we are about to offer may be acceptable to you,
      that it may redeem Holy Mother Church,
      all of us gathered together here,
      all those whom we love or with whom we deal,
      and indeed, all mankind.

CC   We ask, Holy and almighty Father, that you send again now
      your only Son to be the Victim who works our redemption.

All   Yes, with courage in our awe and terror before you,
      we ask you to transform this bread and wine
      into the Body and Blood of Jesus Christ, the Lord.

PC,CC For the Lord Jesus, on the evening before he died,
      took bread, and looking up to heaven,
      to you, his almighty Father,
      he gave you thanks and praise.
      He broke the bread,
      gave it to his disciples and said:
      Take this and eat it, all of you,
      This is my Body,
      which is to be broken for you.
      Whenever you do this,
      do it as a reminder of me.

When supper was ended, he took the cup
again he gave you thanks and praise,
gave the cup to his disciples and said:
Take this and drink from it, all of you:
This is the cup of my Blood,
The Blood of the new and everlasting covenant,
The Mystery of Faith.
This blood is to be shed for you and for all men
so that sins may be forgiven.
Whenever you do this, do it as a reminder of me.

All   So now we remember, we his faithful followers,
the great sacrifice of the Lord,
how he was crucified and died for us,
how he rose gloriously again from death, and
how he ascended into heaven
whence he will come on the day you have appointed
to be judge of all human kind.

CC   We pray that this great work of salvation
may bear fruit today and all days,
making holy the Church,
saving her members from eternal loss.

PC   We pray that all of us gathered here
may have a place one day
with the apostles and martyrs,
as we are now asking to be sharers
in life-giving grace.

CC   We pray, also, that those who have gone before us
in the sign of faith
may have found peace and rest
with you, our God, today and forever.

PC   Through him and in him and with him,
in the unity of the Holy Spirit,
all glory and honor are yours,
Almighty Father,
through all days, forever and ever.

All   Amen, amen, amen, amen.

_____

634 LITURGY OF THE LORD OF LIGHT, Joseph A. Tetlow, S.J.

PC   The Lord be with you.
All   May He be with all of us.
PC   Lift up your hearts.   ← Skip
All   Our hearts are already with the Lord.
PC   We owe thanks to the Lord.
All   Yes, it is only right to thank Him.

PC   Therefore do we thank you and praise you,
   almighty Father,
that you are Light and Wisdom itself
before any other light was.
   We thank you that you have graciously
given us to understand
that you knew yourself, and in the reaches of eternity,
that you shared this understanding with your Son,
only-begotten, God of God, Light of Light,
who is your Wisdom.
   And together you shared the brilliance of your glory
with the Holy Spirit,
who gives witness that your sharing of light
is a sharing of love.
   We thank you, Holy Father,
that from darkness, you brought light;
from chaos, you brought reason and order,
creating the universe a thing of beauty and splendor.
   We thank you
that from unconsciousness, you brought awareness;
and from simple awareness, you brought
comprehension of the world
and knowledge of the self and of others.
   For finally you graced the earth with man,
we who have the light to know ourselves
and each other together,
who can see and acknowledge you
when you show yourself to us,
and freely give our praise to your wisdom and power.
   Therefore we join ourselves to every being
who knows you and bows down before you, crying out to you:

All   Holy, holy, holy.

PC   And though we sin and dim this light,
   you do not abandon us,
faithful and trustworthy Father,
in our darkness, to despair,
but send your Wisdom Himself--the way, the truth,
and the light, to enlighten every man
who comes into the world.

All   Blest is He who comes in the Name of the Lord.
Hosanna in the highest.

PC,CC   For when the time came
which you had appointed,
your Son arose, the light of the world.
He knew what was in the heart of man,
and taught us the true way.
And knowing your will for Himself,
He made the sacrifice of obedience to you,
the sacrifice that was acceptable to you then
as we ask that it be acceptable to you now.

PC **All**   For He it is who offers still to you,
O God of Light,
the clear offering of holding your ways,
the perfect doing your will.
He it is who without fail
did what you asked of Him, giving us the example
which we need but follow to come to you.

PC,CC   For on the night before He died,
knowing fully what was to come to Him,
how He was to give the most perfect teaching
of His new commandment of love
by laying down His life for His friends,
    He took bread, blessed it,
and raising His eyes to heaven to you,
His almighty Father, He gave you thanks and praise.
Then He broke the bread,
gave it to His disciples and said:
Take this and eat it, all of you: this is my Body
    which is to be broken for you.

After dinner was done,
He took the cup, and
handed it around to His disciples, with these words:
This is the cup of my Blood;
a covenant both new and ever-enduring;
the mystery of faith.
This blood is to be spilled for you and for all men
for the forgiveness of sin.
    Then He said: Whenever you do this,
        do it as a memorial of me.

All *PC*   And so it is in memory of your Son,
the Light of the world, that we perform this act.
We recall His life, His death, and His rising,
through which He worked our redemption.

PC,CC   Joined with all the children of light
who have heard and accepted your revelation

through the ages,
joined first with the disciples themselves,
with whom He first shared the light,
then with His holy mother,
and with the martyrs and all the saints;

All   In union, too, with _____, who is our sovereign pontiff,
PC   and with those who are our shepherds,
we ask that this sacrifice be acceptable to you,
Almighty Father,
and that it may profit
all the living,
especially those of us gathered here
and those given into our care;
and the dead,
whom we beg may be brought into the light
of everlasting life.
Through Jesus Christ your Son.

PC   Through Him and with Him and in Him
all glory and honor is yours,
almighty Father,
in union with the Holy Spirit,
from generation to generation,
through all days,
forever and ever.

All   Amen. Amen. Amen.

_____

635 LITURGY OF THE LORD OF LOVE, Joseph A. Tetlow, S.J.

PC   The Lord be with you.

All   May He be with all of us.

PC   Lift up your hearts.

All   Our hearts are already with the Lord.

PC   We owe thanks to God.

All   Yes, it is only right to thank Him.

PC   There are many reasons, almighty and ever-present God,
      why we owe you thanks.
   You are our maker, and the creator of all universes.
   You are our preserver, the mover of time and the energy
      of every act.
   You are our reward, since we trust to be completely happy
      with you forever and ever.

All   For all these reasons, we are grateful to you,
   O Lord our God.

PC   We wish to thank you now especially because you have loved us.
   We did not deserve your love; you gave it to us simply from
      the overflow of your own goodness.
   You loved us first, and have made known to us
   that you choose to be more than maker and preserver,
   that you want to be our Father.
   And you want us to be your sons, serving you
      in a spirit of love, and not in terror and fear.

All   You are many times holy, Lord God of hosts, and
   the earth and the heavens show your splendor and goodness.
   We offer to you higher praise than we give to anyone
      or anything else.

PC   You so loved the world, wanting all men to come to you
   and to be saved from selfishness and fear and sin,
   that you sent to us your only Son.
   He is equal to you in being God, and equal to us in being man.
   He is the sensible proof of your love for us, making us
      co-heirs with Himself of your love.
   And He has taught us that we cannot love you unless we love
      one another as you have loved us,
   making the first move of good will and benevolence
      toward all men without exception.

All   Blest is He who is coming among us in the name of your love.

CC   We are grateful to you that you have taught us by revealing
      your triune life
   that we can give ourselves for the sake of love,
   living our lives for love, even laying down our lives for love,

and still find in this sacrifice of self ourselves,
our place in the family of man, and you yourself.

All   It was your Son who taught us this by giving the final proof
of love by laying down His life to unite His friends
and all men once under your good will and concern.

CC   We are most of all grateful to you, ever-watchful God,
that you have left us a memorial of this sacrifice of your Son.

All   We ask you to make present once again the self-sacrifice
He made.
Find acceptable the memorial we now perform in union
with the whole Church.
May this bread become His body to make us one;
and this wine His blood to join us to Him who is our savior.

PC,CC   For before He died, He took bread, blessed and broke it,
and gave it to His disciples, saying this:
Take this and eat it, all of you.
This is my Body which is to be broken for you.

He also took wine and gave it to His disciples and said:
Take this and drink of it, all of you.
This cup is the cup of my Blood.
It is the sign of a new covenant which will last forever.
It is the mystery of fidelity.
This blood will be spilled for your redemption
and for that of all mankind.
Whenever you do these things, do them as a memorial
of me.

All   We are deeply grateful to you, our Father, that Jesus Christ
your Son commanded us to continue this sign of your perfect
love for us.
In eating this bread and drinking this cup, we are recalling
that your only Son suffered and died for us, and
that he rose from the tomb for us.

PC   Joined with His mother, His disciples, and with the faithful
through the centuries, we rejoice in offering you this sign
of your love.

All   We ask that it help the living and the dead to remain
in your grace and friendship, especially those for whom
we have prayed, and those whom you have given us to love and
to be loved by, and indeed all mankind.
We now ask, God our Father, that through Jesus Christ
present here and now, all honor and praise and glory
might come to you and to the Holy Spirit of love,
from all mankind through all generations and ages
forever and ever.

636   CANON OF JOY, Leonard J. Tighe.

PC   With joy and love, our Father,
we come to this altar of your Son
and rejoice in your invitation
to worship you and express our needs.
As you led the children of Israel
into the land of milk and honey;
so now, we ask you, Father,
lead us by your loving care
into the Paradise prepared for us
so that we may share the Paschal Mystery of Jesus.

CC   In the name of Jesus we thank you, Father,
the lover of men and Creator of all life.
We join hands in this sacrifice of praise and thanksgiving
with all the people of God:
      the suffering, the poor,
      the lonely, the aged,
      the sick, and the joyful.
We ask you to nourish us with the Food of Love,
for we seek in this Banquet of Everlasting Life
the strength to love one another more deeply
and more sincerely than ever before,
to be more open to one another,
and to accept all your children
for what you have made us:
      sons of God.

PC   We need this Food for our pilgrimage to you, Father;
and since we are weary pilgrims on the road to you,
we seek your help.
We keep in mind that Jesus suffered and died for our sins,
that on the third day he rose from the dead,
and that he left our sight to sit at your side
and love all your children:
      his brothers and sisters.
He lives now among us,
in each person, place, and event of our lives.
Draw us all to you in Christ Jesus.

PC,CC Jesus your Son, our Lord and Brother,
on a night of suffering,
gathered to break bread with his loved ones.
He gave you thanks for your fatherly love,
took bread into his hands, broke it,
gave it to his friends, and said:
Take this. Eat it. For it is now my Body,
which is to be broke for you.
Do this in memory of me.

Then he took a cup of wine and gave it to them, saying:
Take this, and drink from this cup.
This is now my Blood, the blood of the New Testament.
It is to be shed for the forgiveness of the sins of all.
Do this in memory of me.

Let us Proclaim the mystery of faith

All We recognize in truth
that this Body and Blood of your Son
is real food and drink.
We rejoice in his promise
that we who eat and drink it
shall never taste of death.
Renew now in our lives the Spirit of Christ,
so that we may go forth
and cry the good news of Jesus Christ with our lives.

CC *P.C.* In the salvation of your people, Our Father,
Jesus brought us a promise of new life:
he destroyed death and crushed the doors of hell
by rising in glory on the third day after his death.
We ask you now to make us into this same Christ;
and, as you sent him into the world
to save it and make all things new,
now send us into the world as his co-workers
to redeem ourselves from past sin
and to bring others to the knowledge and love of him.
We seek the help of the Holy Spirit for this task
and are confident of your constant help and concern.

PC *all* Grant, Father, that we may share
in the banquet of your household on the last day;
for, like the good thief,
we confess him to be
the Son of God.

All *Pc* For it is through him, and with him, and in him,
that we find the way to you, God our Father,
in the joy of the Holy Spirit,
now and to the end of our lives and into eternity.
Amen.

. . . .

THE LORD'S PRAYER IN THE NEW TESTAMENT

Matthew, 6:9-13   Luke, 11:2-4

THE LORD'S PRAYER IN THE NEW TESTAMENT

Mt. 6:9-13   Lk. 11:2-4

698 (The Jerusalem Bible)

Our Father in heaven,   Father, may your name be held
may your name be held holy,   holy,
your kingdom come,   your kingdom come;
your will be done,   give us each day our daily
on earth as in heaven.   bread,
Give us today our daily bread.   and forgive us our sins,
And forgive us our debts,   for we ourselves forgive each
as we have forgiven those   one who is in debt to us.
    who are in debt to us.   And do not put us to the test.
And do not put us to the test,
but save us from the evil one.

699 (Revised Standard Version)

Our Father who are in heaven,   Father, hallowed be thy name.
Hallowed be thy name.   Thy kingdom come.
Thy kingdom come,   Give us each day our daily
Thy will be done,   bread;
    On earth as it is in heaven.   and forgive us our sins, for we
Give us this day our daily   ourselves forgive every one
    bread;   who is indebted to us; and
And forgive us our debts,   lead us not into temptation.
    As we also have forgiven
        our debtors;
And lead us not into temptation,
    But deliver us from evil.

PRAYERS AT THE BREAKING OF THE BREAD

PRAYERS AT THE BREAKING OF THE BREAD

Note: With the introduction of the use of loaves of bread in the Eucharistic Celebration, more emphasis has been placed on the ceremony of the breaking of the bread. This is seen as a significant act of sharing the same food in which the Lord is made known.
James L. Empereur, SJ

---

701   1 Cor. 10:16-17 (RSV)

PC   The cup of blessing which we bless,
is it not a participation in the blood of Christ?
The bread which we break,
is it not a participation in the body of Christ?

All   Because there is one loaf
we who are many are one body,
for we all partake of the same loaf.

---

702   Lk. 24:30-31 (RSV)

PC   When he was at table with them,
he took the bread and blessed and broke it,
and gave it to them.

All   And their eyes were opened
and they recognized him
(in the breaking of the bread).

703

PC   The Lamb of God is broken and distributed
broken but not divided,
ever eaten and never consumed,
sanctifying those who partake of it.
All.   Amen.

---

704   EARLY SOURCES OF THE LITURGY, by Lucien Deiss, C.S.Sp.: "The Euchology of Serapion of Thmius," p. 119.

PC   Make us worthy too to participate in you,
O God of truth,
and grant that our bodies may progress in purity,
our souls in understanding and knowledge.

Give us wisdom, O God of mercies,
through receiving the body and blood (of Christ).

All   Glory to you and power,
through the only-begotten Son,
in the Holy Spirit,
now and for ever and ever.
Amen.

....

PRAYERS AT COMMUNION

PRAYERS AT COMMUNION

Note: The following prayers are suitable for recitation before, or during, or after Communion, as the nature of some of them suggests or as the circumstances seem to require.

---

801 EARLY SOURCES OF THE LITURGY, by Lucien Deiss, C.S.Sp.: "The Apostolic Tradition of Hippolytus of Rome," pp. 44-45.

PC   Let us pray:
Almighty God, make us to be strengthened
by receiving your holy mystery.
Let it not condemn anyone among us
but bless us all through Christ.
Through him, glory to you and power,
now and always
and for all eternity.

All   Amen.

PC   Draw near.
Holy things to the holy!

All   One holy Father alone,
one holy Son alone,
one holy Spirit alone!

PC   The Lord be with you.

All   And with your spirit.

---

802 TRADITIONAL

PC   Holy things for the holy!
One only is holy,
One only is the Lord:
Jesus Christ, to the glory of God the Father.
Come, and receive the Body and Blood of Christ.

---

803 JAMES L. EMPEREUR, S.J.

PC   We give you thanks, God our Father,
for the life and knowledge
you have revealed to us
through Jesus your Son.

All   As the elements of this broken bread
were once scattered on the hillsides,
and being harvested together became one,
so gather your Church together
from the ends of the earth into your kingdom.

PC   We raise the cup of salvation
and call upon the name of the Lord.

All   The cup of blessing for which we give thanks
is the communion of the Blood of Christ.

---

804   LOUIS M. SAVARY, S.J.

PC   The things of God for the People of God.

All   Lord Jesus Christ, you brought life to us
through your death and resurrection.
In gratitude for this freedom
we want to do your will always
and never part from you.
You know our failures in responding to your love.
Yet, trusting in that very love,
we are going to eat your body and drink your blood,
for we wish to live with your life.

PC   The Body and Blood of Christ.

All   Amen.

---

805   Op. cit. #801; pp. 45-46.

PC   Almighty God, Father of the Lord
and our Savior Jesus Christ,
we give you thanks for having granted us
to receive your holy mystery.
Let it not be a cause for us
of fault or of condemnation,
but let it renew soul, body and spirit,
through your only Son.
Through him, glory and power to you,
with him and the Holy Spirit,
now and always,
and for ever.

All   Amen.

The following Scriptural texts are also suggested:

806   Psalm 64 (65), antiphonally with the refrain:
        "We recognize you in the breaking of the bread."

807   Psalm 83 (84), antiphonally as above.

808   Psalm 88 (89), antiphonally as above.

809   Luke, 24:13-35.

810   John, 6:48-69.

811   Ephesians, 2:13-22.

812   Ephesians, 4:4-7, 11-16, 25.

....

DISMISSALS AND BLESSINGS

DISMISSALS AND BLESSINGS

Note: The traditional Roman Liturgy ends with a Postcommunion prayer of thanksgiving for the Gift received, with a final Blessing and dismissal of the congregation. Some of the following may be used as thanksgiving prayers, some as blessings and dismissals.

901 THE BOOK OF COMMON WORSHIP, Provisional Services, p. 45.

PC: Go forth in peace; have courage;
hold onto what is good; return no man evil for evil;
strengthen the fainthearted; support the weak;
help the suffering; honor all men;
love and serve the Lord,
rejoicing in the power of the Holy Spirit.
And may almighty God bless you,
the Father, the Son, and the Holy Spirit.

All Amen.

902

Eternal God, almighty Father of our Lord Jesus Christ,
bless us your servants; protect and help us,
flood us with your life.
May we think the things that are yours,
believe the things that are yours,
and live in peace without giving offense or cause for wrath;
In the name of the Father and of the Son
and of the Holy Spirit.

All Amen.

903 Num. 6:24 (TJB)

PC May Yahweh bless you and keep you.
May Yahweh let his face shine on you and be gracious to you.
May Yahweh uncover his face to you and bring you peace.

904 Adapted from Ps. 120(121):2-8.

PC Our help comes from the Lord.

All Who made heaven and earth.

PC May he never allow you to stumble.

May he sleep not, he who guards over you.
Indeed, he who guards Israel neither sleeps nor slumbers.
The Lord be your guard and your shade at your right side.
The sun shall not harm you, nor the moon.
The Lord guard you from evil;
may he guard your life.
The Lord guard your coming and going
from this time forward and forevermore.

All   Amen.

---

905   Gal. 1:4-5 (TJB)

PC   We wish you the grace and peace of God our Father
and of the Lord Jesus Christ,
who in order to rescue us from this present wicked world
sacrificed himself for our sins,
in accordance with the will of God our Father,
to whom be glory for ever and ever.

All   Amen.

---

906   Phil. 1:9-11 (TJB)

PC   My prayer is that your love for each other
may increase more and more
and never stop improving your knowledge
and deepening your perception,
so that you can always recognize what is best.
This will help you to become pure and blameless,
and prepare you for the Day of Christ,
when you will reach the perfect goodness
which Jesus Christ produces in us
for the glory and praise of God.

All   Amen.

---

907   Phil. 4:4-7 (TJB)

I want you to be happy, always happy in the Lord;
I repeat, what I want is your happiness.
Let your tolerance be evident to everyone:
the Lord is very near.
There is no need to worry;
but if there is anything you need, pray for it,
asking God for it with prayer and thanksgiving,
and that peace of God,
which is so much greater than we can understand,
will guard your hearts and your thoughts, in Christ Jesus.

908 Heb. 13:20-21 (TJB)

PC   I pray that the God of peace,
who brought our Lord Jesus back from the dead
to become the great Shepherd of the sheep
by the blood that sealed an eternal covenant,
may make you ready to do his will in any kind of good action;
and turn us all into whatever is acceptable to himself
through Jesus Christ, to whom be glory for ever and ever.

All   Amen.

---

909 Jude 24-25 (TJB)

PC   Glory be to him who can keep you from falling
and bring you safe to his glorious presence,
innocent and happy.
To God, the only God, who saves us through Jesus Christ
    our Lord,
be the glory, majesty, authority, and power,
which he had before time began,
now and for ever.

All   Amen.

---

910 Rev. 22:20-21 (TJB)

PC   The one who guarantees these revelations
repeats his promise:
I shall indeed be with you soon.

All   Amen; come, Lord Jesus.

PC   May the grace of the Lord Jesus
be with you all.

All   Amen.

....

COMPLETE LITURGIES

<u>Note:</u> Individuals or groups have composed complete (or nearly complete) Ordinaries and Propers for Eucharistic Liturgies to celebrate special events or for the use of specific congregations. A representative sampling of those available to the editor is included as the final section of this book dealing with the Liturgy of the Eucharist.

MASS FOR AN APOSTOLIC GROUP

Robert A. Bagnato, S.J.

<u>Note</u>: Space limitations require some editing of Fr. Bagnato's introductory explanation to this Mass, and do not permit including the detailed and scholarly footnotes with which he documented every statement.

This Mass is one result of a year-long seminar on future liturgies. The participants know how eagerly writers of liturgies look for ideas to open up their horizons. Therefore, we are happy to offer this liturgical formulary to persons who may have occasion to submit experimental Masses to the Bishops' Committee on Liturgical Adaptations and Experimentation for help and approval. We are grateful that our effort now may flow into larger currents of opinion. It is out of the conflict of such opinions that our future liturgies will come forth.

The Mass was designed for a gathering of from five to fifty people. In a group of ten, everyone would have his own role to play. This small group was imagined to be geared to the apostolate, and so apostolic themes were cultivated throughout the Mass.

We have tried to explicitate the advantages of the increased individual participation possible in such a small-group liturgy in the article, "Community vs. Mystery at Mass," in <u>Review for Religious</u>, September 1967. These much-needed benefits cannot be brushed aside flippantly by saying that increased individual participation implies that the role of the priest is reduced to pronouncing the words of consecration. The priest throughout this entire Mass is the visible center, if only because it is he who must weld all the elements into a whole. However, we are quite conscious that too much individual participation must be avoided, since it can produce a dispersion of focus.

Throughout this liturgy biblical images have been used. Likewise because of the religious associations attached to well-known prayers, and also because of the ease with which they can be recited, we have used only the familiar prayers for the responses of the group; e.g. the traditional "Glory to God in the highest."

This liturgy probably would last between twenty-five and thirty minutes, a good length for a weekday Mass. We have tried to avoid repetitions, since each new part added to a Mass can detract from the power and simplicity of what was there before. Moments of silence can be found dispersed throughout the Mass. This gives the participants spiritual room to roam around.

Finally, in passing, we can only mention the continued importance of gesture, attire and surroundings for all the future liturgies. Various parts of the Mass will now be considered briefly:

(1)   This Mass offers an alternative to the much-discussed "open homily," or period of group reflection after the readings. Such a session of group comments could be difficult to sustain daily. In this Mass there are five spontaneous prayers, each at a key point. The prayers need be only two or three sentences, but this personal prayer keeps the entire ceremony personalized. A spontaneous prayer of the faithful or spontaneous petitions at the Mementos are no substitute for these prayers which allow an individual to express his faith-reaction at a critical moment in the Mass.

Since the prayers are pre-assigned, there is less embarassment for beginners who speak - or are silent. On an off-day, even some of these prayers may be dropped.

(2)   This liturgy separates the two readings. The basic principle is that two readings following each other are harder to digest and remember. When the readings are split, each gains in importance and has an opportunity to strike home in its own way and in its own setting.

The Gospel would come first. The second reading is after Communion and serves an entirely different function: with its accompanying spontaneous prayer it forms a brief conclusion and summary for the liturgy, rounding it off and forming a transition to the workaday world. Ultimately, such a delayed reading makes sense only in an atmosphere of spontaneous prayer and within the unique experience of a small-group liturgy, for here greater interpenetration of word and sacrament can be allowed because of the greater unity of the group.

Such a service would be no more inappropriate or anticlimactic than the Postcommunion prayers found in certain proposed liturgies. At any rate, this delayed second reading avoids too abrupt an ending after Communion, which will please some people. Wherever the readings are placed, they must be carefully chosen.

Notice that the celebrant reads an important sentence from each reading before the full text is read. Again, this is to help the group to focus on the readings.

(3)   Fr. Jungmann has pointed out that a public act of penance in the Mass is almost a universal tradition. He lists three spots where this may be found: at the beginning of the Mass, after the liturgy of the word, before the Communion. Jungmann, Kuhn, and Reinhold favor a place after the liturgy of the word, and specifically after the prayer of the faithful. We have put the confession of guilt directly after the Gospel. This emphasizes that it is through the illumination of Christ that we have come to know our culpable lack of love and its abundant forgiveness.

(4)   Notice that we have not eliminated prayers of petition from the Canon, as if the prayers of the faithful can substitute for all intercessory prayers at Mass. However, we have localized in the prayer of the faithful the Mementos of the living and the dead. Here too may be included prayers for the Church.

(5)   The consecration stresses the Eucharist as fulfillment of
the Jewish Passover. Jesus not only changed bread, but the very
ritual life of the people of Israel. Note too that fulfillment is
a theme for the apostolate, and so it is suitable in this Mass for
an apostolic group.

(6)   The Canon has the following outline:
    a. Recall of God's goodness in creation and toward
       Israel.
    b. Group response of praise.
    c. Proclamation of the Christ-event past and present,
       up to and including the present "proclaiming of
       the Lord's death."
    d. Group response of praise.
    e. Prayer begging the Holy Spirit's continued activity
       in the Eucharistic community.
    f. Praise by returning all to the Father, to which is
       added the group "Amen."
We believe that the simplicity and the individual and group participation within the Canon is appropriate in this small-group Mass.
   J.-P. Audet has studied the proper relationships between anam-
nesis (re-enactment), praise, prayer and the participation of the
assembly in the Canon. The interested reader can consult his
works to see how much this Canon has been influenced by his presentation of the traditional pattern underlying the most ancient
Eucharistic formularies.
   Before the consecration, our Canon recites motives for thanks.
There is a definite movement in this narrative, for these motives
stretch from creation through Pentecost, right up to the group's
vocation to be witnesses for Christ and even to its opportunity
now to "proclaim his death." Thus the recitation of the magnalia
Dei is brought up to date, for it includes the very moment of consecration. This is important, for this is why it can be appropriate to have a hymn of praise immediately after God's fresh in-
tervention at the consecration. Then the prayers for the outpour-
ing of the Holy Spirit carry this thrust into the future. The final offering of the Universe (with the risen Christ as its inner-
most core) embraces all of this time and space.

(7)   In the article, "The Holy Spirit and the Eucharist," in
Theological Studies, Fr. Raymond Adams argues convincingly for a
re-examination of the role of the Holy Spirit in Eucharistic theology. He points out that the Spirit received almost no attention
in the Constitution on the Sacred Liturgy. Adams explains why the
salvation roles of Father, Son and Spirit should be recalled ex-
plicitly in the Canon. After all, it is the bond of the Holy Spirit that helps create every Eucharistic community.
   Our own thinking is in line with Adams' article. Toward the
end of the Canon we have placed a prayer, analogous to the epicle-
sis, acknowledging the Holy Spirit as the Spirit of this apostolic
group. By this time in the Mass, consciousness of unity of wor-

ship is very much there within the group. This consciousness of
community is a goal of any Mass. Now is the appropriate moment
for making it explicit in terms of its inner soul, the Holy
Spirit.

(8)   Along with the Roman Rite we have tried to avoid too abrupt a transition from the Canon to the Communion. Therefore, before Communion the commentator dramatically recalls the presiding
presence of Christ himself at his Messianic Banquet. This helps
the group to eat its sacramental meal clustered around the Risen
One.
        We have supposed that Communion under both species would be
allowed in this Mass. We even supposed that the bread might be
in the form of a loaf, and even that the participants, with the
proper care, might be allowed to receive the sacred species in
their hands.

(9)   The celebrant might be allowed discreetly to incorporate
a phrase from the preceding spontaneous prayer into his following
formal prayer. Likewise, the formal prayers might be slightly
modified according to the liturgical season. For variety, alter-
nate prayers could be composed.

In summary, we consider the original contributions of this liturgical formulary to be the following: (1) the extensive possibi- .
lity it gives for active participation by the group and by indivi-
duals; (2) the use of spontaneous individual prayers in all parts
of the liturgy; (3) the cultivation throughout of a specific theme
(the apostolate) for the sake of a specified group.

Other interesting elements of this liturgy are its restructur-
ing of the Canon along simpler and yet traditional lines, its
dramatic setting for Communion, the opportunity it gives to the
celebrant to incorporate an element of previous spontaneous prayer
into this formulary and its use of biblical images. The most radi-
cal feature of this Mass is its challenging of the usual structure
of the liturgy of the word by separating the two readings in an
attempt to re-think this structure within the very different context of a small-group Mass.

Like any newly-imagined liturgy, this one is bound to appear
strange on first reading. A liturgy has to be grown into. Ideal-
ly, a liturgy should evolve with the group. No one liturgy is
ever the perfect answer. If some traditional elements are absent
from this Mass, it is not because we despise our heritage. Rather
we confess that our ingenuity is unable to combine, into a harmo-
nious whole within one Mass, all the elements of our tradition.
Even an anthology of liturgies still cannot articulate fully the
many facets of the Eucharistic mystery. However, striving to
bring out the many sides of the tradition on the Mass is part of
this tradition itself.

_____

A MASS WITH BIBLICAL THEMES FOR AN APOSTOLIC GROUP

Liturgy of the Word

(The Mass may begin with an opening hymn.)
(There is a moment of recollection and silence.)
(There is a spontaneous prayer by one of the group.)
(Slight pause.)

PC   (Reads an important sentence from the first reading.)

PC   Glory be to the Father,
All   and to the Son, and to the Holy Spirit...etc....

PC   (Again reads the verse from the first reading.)

(A participant reads the Gospel, from the altar or from a lectern.)

(Spontaneous prayer by one of the group, based on the Gospel.)
(Slight pause.)

PC   (Again reads the selected verse from the first reading.)

Commentator: Christ Jesus,
    your Gospel is the Light of the world.
    We repent of ever having turned to darkness.
    You are the Yes that confirms all God's promises.
    We are sorry that we shrink back from your Father's love.
    You are the Model Shepherd.
    May we not again speak with a stranger's voice to your flock.

PC   Lamb of God,
All   who take away the sins of the world,...etc....

PC   If any of us does fall into sin,
        we have an advocate to plead our cause
        before the Father
        in the Just One, Jesus Christ.
        He more than carries our sins,
        and not only ours,
        but the sins of the whole world.
        Therefore, let us have confidence
        as we now enter the sanctuary
        through the blood of Jesus,
        through the risen and living way.

(The celebrant takes his place at the altar.)
(There may be a prepared or spontaneous prayer of the faithful.)
(There may be a moment of silence for further personal intentions
    for the living and dead.)
(The following concluding prayer may be used:)

PC   Father, we pray along with your saints -
our mother, Mary, - St. Joseph, the first apostles,
the martyrs throughout the centuries,
all the saints alive today throughout your Church:
Father, may your Kingdom come, may your will be done.
Send your Spirit to those who ask you.

Liturgy of the Eucharist

(There may be an offertory hymn.)
(A participant gives a spontaneous offertory prayer.)
(The celebrant pours water into the wine.)
(During the following prayer and response, the celebrant extends
   his arms at full length to include all the people:)

PC   Brethren, pray that our living sacrifice
may be acceptable to God our Father almighty.

All   May the Lord receive the sacrifice from your hands,
to the praise and glory of his name,
for our welfare and that of all his holy Church.

Eucharistic Prayer

PC   The Lord be with you.
All   And with your spirit.
PC   Lift up your hearts.
All   We have lifted them up to the Lord.
PC   Let us give thanks to the Lord our God.
All   It is right and just.

(Note: In the following P1=Participant I)

P1   Give thanks to the Lord, for he is great.
All   (perhaps singing:) For his great love is without end.

P1   Give thanks to the Lord, for he is good.
All   For his great love is without end.

P1   He formed the earth to be inhabited.
All   For his great love is without end.

P1   He created man in his own image,
male and female he created them.
All   For his great love is without end.

P1   With a mighty hand, he led Israel out of Egypt
to serve him.
All   For his great love is without end.

P1   Give thanks to the Lord all your life,
for now behold he has done a new thing.

All   For his great love is without end.

P1   We give you thanks and praise, Loving Father,
        that the prophecies have been fulfilled,
        that the New Age has been inaugurated
        by the sending of your Son.
      He is the first-born of all creation.
        All was created through him and for him.
        In him all things hold together.
      Born of Mary, Jesus lived our life,
        and grew in wisdom, stature and grace.
      He is the first-born from the dead,
        a life-giving Spirit.
        He has poured out this promised Spirit upon his Church.
      It is through him that we have received the grace of apostle-
            ship.
        All over the world men must be taught to honor his name
        by paying him the homage of their faith.
      May we preach to men
        what they worship as unknown.
        May we proclaim his death, until he comes.

PC   Before that Paschal feast began,
      Jesus already knew that the time had come
      for his passage from this world to the Father.
      He had loved those who were his own in the world,
      and he loved them to the last.
      He said to them, "I have longed and longed
      to eat this Paschal meal with you before my passion."
      For Jesus was about to fulfill the Passover supper.

      (The celebrant takes the bread.)

PC,CC While they were still there at table,
      Jesus took bread, gave thanks to his Almighty Father,
      broke the bread and gave it to his friends, as usual,
      but he said:
      "Take this and eat.
      This is my Body, given up for you."

      (The celebrant elevates the Sacred Species, and genu-
      flects. Then he takes the chalice.)

      When that supper was ended, he took the cup,
      in the usual way offered thanks,
      and gave the cup to his friends, but with the words:
      "Take this and drink, all of you;
      for this is the cup of my Blood,
      the Blood of the new and everlasting covenant,
      the mystery of faith,
      to be poured out for you and all others,
      to obtain the forgiveness of sins.

And I tell you this,
I shall not drink of this fruit of the vine again,
until I drink it with you, new wine,
in the Kingdom of my Father."

(The celebrant elevates the chalice and genuflects.)

PC   Our Passover is sacrificed. It is Christ himself.
       Glory to God in the highest.
All   and on earth peace to men of good will,...etc....

(Spontaneous prayer by one of the group.)

CC   Father, may the Holy Spirit from this Eucharist,
       guide us into all truth.
       May this Spirit make us comprehend the love of Christ
       which surpasses knowledge.
       May our group Spirit guide us out all over the world
       to preach Christ's gospel to the whole creation.

(The celebrant elevated both Sacred Species, saying:)

PC   In him, and through him, and with him,
       here, even now, despite our sinfulness, Father,
       we are returning to you all your universe
       forever and ever.
All   Amen.

Communion

Commentator: Jesus came and stood among them
    and said to them, "Peace be with you."
When he had said this, he showed them his hands and his side.
Then the disciples were glad when they saw the Lord.

(The celebrant, holding out the Sacred Species, with the
loaf over the chalice, turns to all around the altar as
he says:)

PC   May the peace and gladness of our gracious risen Lord
       now be with you.
All   And with your spirit.

(While the celebrant is breaking the loaf for distri-
bution, the commentator says:)

Commentator: We know what love means
    from the fact that he laid down his life for us.
So we also ought to lay down our lives for our brothers.

(The broken loaf is distributed to all. When all have a

piece of the loaf in their hands, the Commentator says:)

Commentator: He stood in the midst of them and said,
   "It is myself. Handle me and see."
And while they still disbelieved for joy, he asked,
   "Have you anything here to eat?"
He took and ate in their presence,
and shared his meal with them.

        (All eat.)

        (The celebrant and the people drink from the chalice.
        As they drink, the commentator says:)

Commentator: I am the vine, you are the branches.
   He who abides in me, and I in him,
   he it is that bears much fruit,
   for apart from me you can do nothing.
   Every branch that does bear fruit
   my Father prunes, that it may bear still more fruit.

        (After all have drunk from the chalice, the priest puri-
        fies it and the paten sufficiently to consume the rest of
        the Sacred Species.)

        Conclusion

        (A Communion hymn is sung.)

PC   (Reads an important sentence from the second reading.)

(Someone gives the second reading.)

(Spontaneous, concluding prayer by a participant, perhaps based on
   the second reading.)
(Slight pause)

PC   (Gives his final blessing, perhaps incorporating into it a
       theme for the final spontaneous prayer.)

———————————————————

AN EXPERIMENTAL LITURGY FOR YOUNG ADULTS

David L. Cooke, S.J.

General Confession:

PC   In the name of the Father, and of the Son,
     and of the Holy Spirit.
All Amen.

All   God our Father, at your invitation
     we have come together as one family.
         We come not in fear, but in trust and confidence,
     because of your great goodness.
         We confess that we have done wrong
     by not caring when we should have cared,
     by our indifference to the needs of parents and friends,
     by hating and ignoring those not in our crowd,
     by misusing your gifts of love and friendship.
         Through the mercy and goodness of Christ our Lord
     forgive us for not doing the good you command,
     and for doing the evil you forbid.
     Restore peace and joy to our hearts;
     set our minds on justice and love:
     so that one in spirit we may grow to full sonship
     and bring peace to the world in which we live.

PC   May the almighty and merciful God grant us pardon, absolution,
     and remission of our sins.
All Amen.

Thematic Prayer:

PC   The risen Christ be with you.
All And with you also.
PC   Let us pray: (spontaneous prayer based on theme of Mass)

Readings: (chosen according to theme of Mass)

Creed:

PC   Let us stand and together profess our faith in
     the three divine persons: Father, Son, and Holy Spirit.

All   I believe in God the Father
     who created the heavens and the earth,
     who makes the sun to rise upon the just and the unjust,
     who provides for and protects all men as his children.
         I believe that the Father so loved the world
     that he sent his only Son for our salvation.

I believe in Jesus Christ as Son
who for love of us became man,
who accepted our human condition,
who experienced our humanity
with its joys and sorrows,
its disappointments and expectations.
    I believe that in facing and accepting death
at the hands of sinful mankind and in rising to a new life
he won for us our salvation.
    I believe that the Father and the Son
have sent their own Spirit to us.
    I believe in the Holy Spirit as Giver of Life
who vivifies our spirit,
who unites us in peace and charity,
who forms us into the one community of God.
    I believe that the Father, Son, and Holy Spirit
send us into the world in witness
and in service to our fellow man.

Prayer of the Faithful:

PC   The risen Christ be with you.
All   And with you also.
PC   Let us pray: (intentions of PC and All)

Prayer Over the Gifts:

PC   Accept, Holy Father, this bread and wine
      as sign and symbol of ourselves.
Sanctify these gifts with the personal presence of your Son
      through the transforming action of your Spirit.
May this bread which is food
      become nourishment and strength for us,
And may this wine which is drink
      become joy and peace for us
      in building up your family on earth.

Eucharistic Prayer:

PC   The risen Christ be with you.
All   And with you also.
PC   Let us raise our hearts and minds to the Father.
All   And with our Lord Jesus Christ let us thank him
      for his goodness.

    (Cf. #609, p. 52.)

Eucharistic Banquet:

PC   With one voice and one heart let us pray to the Father
      as Jesus taught us to pray:

All	Our Father in heaven, blessed be your name.

All Our Father in heaven, blessed be your name.
your kingdom come, your will be done
on earth as in heaven.
Give us this day our daily bread,
and forgive us our sins
as we forgive those who wronged us.
And bring us not to hard testing,
but deliver us from evil.

Sign of Peace:

PC God, our Father, you have sent peace into this world
through Christ your Son.
Grant that the sign of peace which we now give to each other
may be a sign of our at-one-ness with you
and of our friendship with each other
so that we may bring your peace to those we live with;
this we ask through Christ our Lord.

All Amen. May the peace of the risen Christ be with you.

Communion:

PC Because there is one loaf, we who are many are one body,
for all partake of the one loaf which is Christ.

All May the Body of our Lord Jesus Christ nourish and
strengthen us into life everlasting.

PC The cup of blessing which we bless,
is a participation in the life of Jesus.

All May the Blood of our Lord Jesus Christ
unite us into life everlasting.

Final Dismissal:

PC Live joyfully and gratefully
by the strength of this heavenly food,
sharing in the death and resurrection of the Lord.
Fill the world with the Spirit of Christ,
and in all things,
in the very midst of human affairs,
become a witness of Christ.
And may Almighty God bless you,
the Father, Son, and Holy Spirit.

All Amen.

A WEDDING LITURGY

David L. Cooke, S.J.

Entrance Song: "This Is The Day"

PC We have come to celebrate the Banquet of Life
which Christ has given us in the Eucharist
and to witness the Feast of Love
which _____ and _____ are to share in marriage.
Let us begin by reminding ourselves
that love must be a part of our lives,
and let us kneel to confess
that we have not loved enough.

Confession:

All Father, your Son has shown us how to love
and invites us to love one another
as he loves us. We confess that our lives
have not been a fulfillment of this.

We have been proud and selfish, impatient with others,
and all too accommodating to ourselves.
We have not trusted enough in your love
and in the love of each other.

We have not been open with each other, afraid
to take the chance that in loving we may not be
loved in return.

There are times when we have had the opportunity
to make love for one another a reality, and
we have remained silent.

Father, pardon the unkind word,
the impatient gesture,
and the selfish deed.

Forgive our failure to become involved
in the needs of others.

Grant that we may walk always in your presence
so as to arrive at the fullness of life.

Hymn of Praise

Prayer

Readings:

First Reading - 1 Jn. 4:7-12, 16

Gradual Response: 1 Cor. 13:4-7

Second Reading - Jn. 15:1-8

Homily

Creed:

All   We believe that Jesus Christ is the Son of God,
        and that God has given us eternal life in his Son.
      We believe that Jesus is the Resurrection and the Life,
        and that whoever believes in him shall live.
      We believe that God is Spirit,
        and that we must worship him in spirit and in truth.
      We believe that God is Light,
        and that if we walk in the light,
        we have fellowship with one another.
      We believe that God is Love,
        and that everyone who loves
        is born of God and knows God.
      We believe that where the Spirit of the Lord is,
        there is the Church of Christ.

Wedding Creed and Vows:

Bride and Groom
      We believe that by our love we bear witness
        to the union of Christ and his Church.
      We believe that we are meant to be for each other
        a sign of Christ's love.
      We believe that we are called to bring each other to God.
      We believe that we are called to build up
        the family of God here on earth.
      We believe that we are meant to give our children
        in service to God and mankind.

Groom   Believing these things, _____,
        I offer myself to you completely
        to be your husband in marriage.

Bride   I accept you as my husband,
        and believing as you do, _____,
        I offer myself to you completely
        to be your wife in marriage.

Groom   I accept you as my wife,
        and call upon the Christian community
        to witness our union.

Both   With the witness of this community,
      we offer ourselves together
      as man and wife to God.

Witnesses   We have heard _____ and _____ pledge themselves
to each other and to God in marriage.
Before God and this community,
we testify that _____ and _____
are now husband and wife, one flesh.

PC   By the authority of the Church I ratify and bless
the bond of marriage you have contracted.
In the name of the Father and of the Son
and the Holy Spirit.

Blessing and Giving of the Rings

Prayers of the Faithful:

PC   That the love of _____ and _____,
which has drawn them together
and led them to enter this marriage,
may grow stronger in their life together,
we pray to the Lord.

All   Lord, hear our prayer. (Response to each prayer by PC.)

PC   That this Christian marriage may begin with joy
and endure in peace.....

That all present may be inspired
by the love of this Christian couple,
and by the faith in the future
that enables them to begin a new family in the Church.....

That all present may find renewed joy and peace
in their families through this celebration.....

By the grace of the Holy Spirit, God,
you pour into the hearts of all men
the gift of the ability to love.
Grant a generous increase of this gift
to this couple and to the community,
so that they may be known by their love,
through Christ our Lord. Amen.

Kiss of Peace:

(At this time the community is invited to gather around the altar.)

Offertory Song: "Take Our Bread"

Offertory Prayer:

PC   Together with these offerings of bread and wine,
O God, we give you our hearts and our minds,

and all that we are.
By the power of the body and blood of Jesus,
    which we will receive here together,
    let us feel the faith which each of us has in you,
    so that we may encourage one another
    to take your Son into our lives
    as our one and true savior and brother,
    Jesus Christ, our Lord. Amen.

Eucharistic Prayer: John L'Heureux, S.J.; cf. #629, p. 97.

Our Father

Nuptial Blessing

Communion Prayer:

PC,All   Because there is one loaf, we who are many are one body,
              for all partake of the one loaf.
          May the Body of our Lord Jesus Christ
              nourish and strengthen us
              unto life everlasting. Amen.

          The cup of blessing which we bless,
              is it not a participation in the Blood of Christ?
          May the Blood of our Lord Jesus Christ
              unite us unto life everlasting. Amen.

Communion Song: "God Is Love"

Prayer

Final Blessing:

PC   Live joyfully and gratefully
      by the strength of his heavenly food,
      sharing in the death and resurrection of the Lord.
      Fill the world with the Spirit of Christ,
      and in all things, and in the very midst
      of human affairs, become a witness of Christ.

          Recessional Song: "They'll Know We Are Christians"

- 145 -

LITURGY OF THE LIBERATION OF THE SOUL

Robert R. Dwelley

PC   In the name of the Father, Son, and Holy Spirit.
All   Amen.

Entrance Hymn: Ps. 14:1, 2, 5; Ps. 17:7 (CCD).

All   O Lord, who shall sojourn in your tent?
Who shall dwell on your holy mountain?
He who walks blamelessly and does justice...
shall never be disturbed.
In my distress I called upon the Lord
and cried out to my God;
from his temple he heard my voice,
and my cry to him reached his ears.
    Glory be to God the Father, Son, and Holy Spirit.
    He always was, is now, and will be forever. Amen.

Confession of Sins:

PC   God has promised us forgiveness of sins if only we truly repent.
Let us consider our wrongdoings and ask
another chance to prove our love for him.

All   I confess to almighty God,
to the Virgin Mary,
to all the saints,
and to all of you, my brothers,
that I have sinned grievously through my own negligence.
I humbly beg forgiveness.

PC   May almighty God have mercy on us and forgive us our sins,
in the name of the Father, Son, and Holy Spirit.
All   Amen.

Hymn of Praise:

All   Glory to God on high and peace to all men on earth.
We give praise, blessing, worship, and thanksgiving
    to the Father,
    to his Son who died for us, and
    to the Holy Spirit.
Only you are holy, O God.
Only you are the Lord.
Only you are the most high.
And you will live forever. Amen.

Entrance Prayer:

PC   May the Lord always live with you.

All   And with you, too.

PC   Let us pray: Almighty God, you have chosen to take from among
      us through death people whom we love.   Teach us not to grieve
      in this, but to rejoice; for by death the imperfections and in-
      firmities of the body are shed and we share eternal happiness
      in the sight of you.   We ask you this realization through our
      brother, Jesus Christ, who, together with the Holy Spirit, is
      one God with you forever.

All   Amen.

      First Reading: Rev. 14:13 (by a member of the congregation).

      Second Reading: Jn. 6:51-55 (by the Celebrant).

      Meditation Hymn: Ps. 16:4-5, 15 (CCD).

All   My mouth has not transgressed after the manner of man;
      according to the words of your lips I have kept the ways
         of the law.
      My steps have been steadfast in your paths,
      my feet have not faltered.
      I in justice shall behold your face;
      on waking, I shall be content in your presence.

(Homily, or group discussions of insights into the readings.)

      Creed:

All   I believe that there is only one God,
      and in this God there are three distinct persons:
         the Father, who made all things in heaven and on earth;
         his Son, Jesus Christ, who was born of a virgin,
            who lived a human life while remaining God,
            and who died for our sins;
         and also the Holy Spirit, who proceeds from the intense
            love between the Father and the Son.
      I also believe that the Catholic Church is the one,
         true Church that God instituted.
      In this Church he gives us spiritual life and forgiveness
         for our sins.
      I am waiting for the dead to come back to life on the
            last day,
         and for an eternal life which follows this one. Amen.

      Prayer of the Faithful: (intentions of the congregation)

      Offertory Hymn: Jn. 6:52, 55 (CCD).

All   Christ said: "I am the living bread which came down from
      heaven. He who eats it will live forever. Yes, whoever
      feeds on my flesh and drinks my blood has

- 147 -

eternal life, and I will raise him up on the last day."

Offering of the Gifts:

(Each places his offering of bread onto the paten, and the priest
gives it to God in the name of all Christians:)

PC   Take this bread and wine, Father, which we offer you
as a sign of the gift of ourselves to you.
We trust that this sacrifice will glorify you,
give the saints honor, and help us to salvation.

And you, brothers, pray that God will accept our sacrifice.

All   Take these gifts we offer you, O Lord,
so that your name will be praised
throughout the world forever. Amen.

Prayer Over the Gifts:

PC   Dear God, we give you these things on behalf of all those who
have died. Look kindly on this sacrifice so that we also may
receive the rewards of supernatural life. We ask this through
Jesus Christ and the Holy Spirit. They are one God with you
forever.

All   Amen.

Preface and Canon:

All   Let us lift up our hearts, our minds, our very being to God
so that we can worthily accept his love.

PC   Remember that we will all die.
It is inevitable, but it need not be the occasion for sadness,
because for those who are faithful to God's ways
life is not ended but only changed.
For this reason we should be happy about death.
When a person dies, the restrictions and discomforts
of the human body are dissolved,
and our immortal parts enjoy the sight of God.
Preparing ourselves for this change, then,
let us join together with all of God's creation,
and in loud, joyful voices say:

All   Holy is the Lord God,
who fills all of heaven and earth with his power and glory.
Rejoice and be happy, for he has promised us
salvation and eternal life if we are faithful.

PC   This sacrifice is being offered for all Christians,
living and dead,
whom God has blessed with the gifts of life and faith.

- 148 -

All   Christ underwent death, as each of us will;
and his death was joyous, because by it we were redeemed.
In order to share intimately with God
the delights of eternal life,
we, too, must follow the example of Christ,
carry our own crosses as best we can, and then die.
In leaving our bodies behind,
our souls are freed to live forever with God.

PC,CC Christ left us a commemoration of his death
when, on that first Holy Thursday,
he took bread into his hands
and gave it to those at the table, saying:
"Eat this, because it is my Body."

He also passed around a chalice of wine, saying:
"Drink from this chalice, because it is my Blood
which is going to be shed for all men
so that their sins may be forgiven."

Then he made his sacrifice eternal, by saying:
"I want you to do these things to remember me."

Let us proclaim the mystery of Faith.

All   Now that we have done these things,
we give through Christ
all honor and glory
to the Father and Holy Spirit
forever. Amen. *Sung.*

Ceremony of Peace - Communion:

PC   Let us now make as close a partnership with Christ's life
and death by taking the food he himself gave us.
To do so worthily, we must first reconcile ourselves
to each of our neighbors.
Let us greet each other in the peace, love, and joy of Christ.

(Everyone greets his neighbors with an outward sign that he wishes
Christ to be with that person. The Celebrant then gives the Eucharist to each in the Christian name of his Baptism.)

Communion Hymn: Ps. 22 (CCD). — *during Communion*

All   The Lord is my shepherd; I shall not want.
In verdant pastures he gives me repose;
beside restful waters he leads me;
He refreshes my soul.
He guides me in right paths for his name's sake.
Even though I walk in the dark valley,
I fear no evil; for you are at my side
with your rod and your staff that give me courage.

You spread the table before me in the sight of my foes;
you anoint my head with oil; my cup overflows
Only goodness and kindness follow me all the days
   of my life;
and I shall dwell in the house of the Lord for years
   to come.

The Lord's Prayer:

PC   Now let us pray to God the way Christ our Brother taught us.

All   Our Father, who are in heaven,.....

Prayer After Communion:

PC   O God, now that we have accepted the sacrament you offered us,
      Help us to live our lives according to what you want. Then,
      when we die, we will live again forever. This we ask of you
      through Jesus Christ and the Holy Spirit, who are one and the
      same God with you, forever.
All   Amen.

Blessing and Dismissal:

PC   God has promised us eternal life if we do his will.
      Let us ask his blessing, so that we may live good lives.

All   God bless all of us,
      through the Father, Son, and Holy Spirit. Amen.

PC   The Eucharist is ended and begun.
      Go now in the peace, joy, and love of Christ.
All   Thanks be to God.

_____

AN EXPERIMENTAL LITURGY

James L. Empereur, S.J.

PC is vested in stole and alb. (Liturgy of the Word could be conducted by a Deacon.) Gifts are prepared on the altar or on a side
table. Liturgy of the Word is conducted away from the altar. All
stand around the Celebrant.

LITURGY OF THE WORD

Opening: A hymn can be sung. Depending upon the situation,
this hymn could be begun before all have arrived and the people
could join in as they enter the room. After the hymn, or in the
beginning, if there is no hymn, PC announces the theme and begins:

PC   In the name of the Father and the Son and the Holy Spirit,
All Amen.
PC   Our help is in the name of the Lord,
All Who made heaven and earth.

General Confession: cf. #201, by Roger Kuhn, p. 5.

(When appropriate, the confession can be replaced by the Hymn
of Praise following. Both can be used in the same liturgy.

PC   Glory to God on high.
All Peace on earth and God's good will to men.
     We praise you, we bless you, we worship you, we glorify you.
     We thank you for showing us your great glory.
     Lord God, King of heaven, almighty God our Father.
     Lord Jesus Christ, only-begotten Son,
     Lord God, Lamb of God, Son of the Father.
     You take away the sins of the world: have mercy on us.
     You take away the sins of the world: accept our prayer.
     You are seated at the right hand of the Father:
        have mercy on us.
     You alone are the Holy One.
     You alone are the Lord.
     You alone are the most high, Jesus Christ,
     with the Holy Spirit
     in the glory of God the Father. Amen.

Thematic Prayer:

PC   The Lord be with you.
All And also with you.
PC   Let us pray: (The prayer, usually extemporaneous, should be
     connected with both the immediate situation and with the theme
     of the Mass.)
All Amen.

Readings; Homily: (A lector reads a passage from Scripture, related to the theme of the day. Selections from any appropriate work may be read so long as they are relevant, so long as the Gospel itself is from one of the four Gospels. There may be one or several readings. All are seated for the readings, even when the Gospel is read; although the reader may stand if the situation requires.

After the reading(s), anyone present may offer reflections; or, if the group lends itself to this, spontaneous prayers.)

Intercessory Prayers:

PC   Let us pray for: (PC and then all present, or as many as want to, mention the intentions for which they wish the group to pray. It seems natural to begin each intention with "Let us pray for"; it seems natural also for the group not to make a response after each intention.)

PC   (offers a summary prayer for the intentions, including reference to the theme of the day or to the liturgical season.)

Prayer for Peace and Unity:

PC   Let us pray before we greet one another in peace.
All   Almighty Father, Ruler of the universe,
look down upon your Church,
upon all your people,
and upon this group assembled here,
and save all of us, your unworthy servants,
and give us your peace, your love, and your assistance.
Send down upon us the free gift of your Holy Spirit
so that with clean heart and good conscience
we may love one another,
not deceitfully nor hypocritically,
not to control each other's freedom,
but blamelessly and purely in the bonds of peace and love.
Loving each other in this way,
let us all come to you and to your infinite love
through Jesus Christ our Lord
with the Holy life-giving Spirit
now and through endless ages. Amen.

(Here, if it is a natural gesture, PC and All exchange the ritual kiss of eaace.)

LITURGY OF THE EUCHARIST

Offertory: (The group can sing a hymn as transition between the Liturgy of the Word and the Liturgy of the Eucharist. PC now puts on the chasuble; CC puts on alb, cincture, stole; a candle is lighted; all approach the altar.

To avoid giving undue emphasis to the offertory, the gifts are already prepared on the altar; PC may merely uncover them or may say some spontaneous prayer voicing his intention to consecrate this bread and this wine to the honor and glory of God and to the union of him in the group present.

PC   (inviting all to come to the Eucharistic table:)
        Luke the Evangelist writes of our Risen Lord that,
        when he was at table with them,
        he took bread and blessed and broke it and gave it to them.
        And their eyes were opened and they recognized him.
        This is Christ's table.
        Our Savior invites those who love him
        to share the feast he has prepared.
        Let us open our hearts to one another
        as Christ has opened his heart to us,
        and God will be glorified.
        The peace of the Lord Jesus Christ be with you all.
All   And also with you.

        Eucharistic Prayer: cf. pp. 34-115.

        Communion (PC breaks the bread and gives a portion to those who wish to communicate. Then, holding his own host, he says:)

PC   We give you thanks, Father, for the life and knowledge
        you have sent us through Jesus, your Son.
        As the elements of this broken bread were once scattered
            on the mountains,
        and being gathered together became one,
        so gather your Church together from the ends of the earth
        into your kingdom.
All   Amen.
        (All consume together.)
PC   We give you thanks, Father, for your holy name
        and for the faith and immortality you have sent us
        through Jesus, your Son. To you be glory forever.
        (PC raises the chalice)
        Let us raise the cup of salvation and call upon the name
            of the Lord.
        The cup of blessing for which we give thanks
        is the communion of the Blood of Christ.
All   Amen.
        (All drink from the chalice. A psalm may be recited during this time or a hymn may be sung.)

        (When all have received, PC invites all to pray "The Lord's Prayer"; or it may be sung.)

PC   (says a Postcommunion prayer, perhaps drawing together the
        comments from the readings.)

        (PC may ask for final comments on the theme, but only if the group is very close and very communicative.)

<u>Dismissal:</u>

PC   Go out into the world in peace; have courage; hold on to what
        is good;
     return no man evil for evil; strengthen the fainthearted;
        support the weak;
     help the suffering; honor all men; love the unloved;
     serve the Lord, rejoicing in the power of the Holy Spirit.

     The Lord bless you and keep you.
     The Lord make his face shine upon you and be gracious to you.
     The Lord lift up his countenance upon you and give you peace.

     And may almighty God bless you(us):
     the Father, and the Son, and the Holy Spirit.

<u>All</u>   Amen.

(Ablutions may be conducted after the liturgy if that seems
better.)

- 154 -

LITURGY ON THE DAY OF CHRISTIAN BURIAL

Note: Parts of this liturgy are reprinted from a provisional translation of the experimental rite of funerals prepared by the post-conciliar commission for the reform of the liturgy and reprinted here with permission of the owner, the International Committee on English in the Liturgy, Inc., for study purposes only.

(A) - IN THE CHURCH

LITURGY OF THE WORD

1. Blessing of Body: Celebrant greets family, friends at entrance of church, then turns to body. Blessing body with holy water, he says:

PC   Welcome, Christian servant, our brother/sister in the Lord, you who have fallen asleep in Christ and now rest in his peace. In the Temple you entered the community of faith. Here in union with your brothers and sisters, you nourished your Christian life and grew in oneness with Jesus Christ. We welcome you here this one last time to bid you farewell until we are all together again in the glory which Christ has won for us.

2. Procession into Church: can be led by cross or paschal candle which is then placed near coffin. Hymn is sung during procession.

3. Greetings and Prayer:

PC   We bless the God and Father of our Lord Jesus Christ, the Father of mercy, and the God of comfort, who comforts us in our afflictions. Let us trust in God, for he will help us through his Son who invites us: "Come to me all you who labor and are burdened, and I will give you rest."

PC,All   Lord, have mercy.....

PC   The Lord be with you!
All   And with your spirit!

PC   Our brother/sister has fallen asleep in the peace of Christ. In the faith and hope of eternal life, let us command him/her to the most loving mercy of our Father. Let our prayers go with him/her that he/she, who by Baptism became one of God's children and who so often stood to be fed at the Lord's table, may now be summoned to the table of God's family in heaven. With the saints may he/she inherit the everlasting promise.

Let us pray also for ourselves: in time to come may we, who

now mourn and weep, be able to go with our brother/sister to meet Christ when he himself who is our life shall appear in his glory.

(Pause for silent prayer.)

Lord, holy Father, All-powerful, everlasting God, we humbly pray for the soul of your servant _____ whom you have bidden to come to you from this life. Be pleased to grant him/her a place of cool repose, of light and peace. May he/she pass through the gates of death and remain in the dwelling of the saints and in that holy light which from of old you promised to Abraham and his children. May his/her soul suffer no harm; but on that great day of resurrection and reward, be pleased to raise him/her with your saints and your chosen ones. Pardon all his/her faults and sins; and let him/her come to immortal life with you in the eternal kingdom. We ask this through our Lord Jesus Christ your Son, who lives and reigns with you in the unity of the Holy Spirit, God, forever and ever.

All   Amen.

4. First Reading: Rom. 8:12-23.

(It is also possible to use one of the following readings: 1 Cor. 15:51-57, 12-22; 1 Thess. 4:13-18; 2 Cor. 5:1-10; Rev. 14:12-13; 21:2-5;   2 Cor. 4:10-5:1.)

5. Gospel: Jn. 12:23-28.

(It is also possible to use one of the following readings: Jn. 5:25-29; 6:35-55; 11:1-45; 12:23-28; 14:1-6; 17:24-26; Mt. 25:31-46; Lk. 12:35-40; 16:19-31; 23:39-43.)

6. Homily

7. Prayer of the Faithful:

PC   The Lord be with you!
All   And with your spirit!

PC   God our almighty Father has raised Christ his Son from the dead. Let us therefore call upon him with confidence to save the living and the dead:

PC or L   That our brother/sister _____, given the seed of immortal life in Baptism, may be granted eternal fellowship with the saints, let us pray to the Lord:

All   Lord, hear our prayer.

PC or L   That he/she may be raised up on the last day, for the Body of Christ, the Bread of Eternal Life, has been his/her food, let us pray to the Lord:
All   Lord, hear our prayer.

PC or L   That God may welcome into the light of his presence all
          who have died in the hope of resurrection, let us pray to
          the Lord:

All   Lord, hear our prayer.

PC or L   For all of us whom our brother/sister has left behind,
          that we too may someday pass from death to life, to the
          joy that will never end, let us pray to the Lord:
All   Lord, hear our prayer.

LITURGY OF THE EUCHARIST

1. Prayer Over the Gifts: Celebrant goes to altar to prepare
   gifts. Then:

PC   Lord our Father, hear our prayers for the soul of your
      servant _____ and accept the gifts that we present to you.
      Through this sacrifice of praise which we are offering,
      grant him/her fellowship with your saints. Through Jesus
      Christ your Son who lives and reigns with you in the unity
      of the Holy Spirit, God, for ever and ever.
All   Amen.

2. Eucharistic Prayer

3. Communion Service

4. Thanksgiving Prayer:

PC   The Lord be with you!
All   And with your spirit!
PC   Let us pray now in thanksgiving:
          (Pause for silent prayer.) ——>
      Most merciful Father, into your hands we commend the soul of
      our brother/sister _____, for we are sustained by the sure
      hope that he/she will rise again on the last day with all
      those who have died in Christ.
      We give you thanks for all the good things you gave your ser-
      vant in this mortal life as signs for us of your goodness and
      of the communion of saints in Christ. Lord, in your great
      pity accept our prayer that the gates of paradise may be
      opened for our brother/sister.
      In our turn, may we too be comforted by the words of faith
      until we hasten to meet Christ when we may all be forever
      with the Lord and with our brother/sister.
      Through our Lord Jesus Christ your Son, who lives and reigns
      with you in the unity of the Holy Spirit, God, for ever and
      ever.
All   Amen.

PC   As is the custom of believers, we bring the human body to

burial. To God all living things are bound. Let us pray
that he/she will rise again to new life and take his/her
place with those who have won the victory of Christ.
May God grant him/her mercy when he/she is judged.
May he/she be redeemed from death and forgiven his/her sins.
May he/she live at peace with the Father and enjoy forever
the company of the saints.

All   Amen.

5. The Blessing

PC   And may Almighty God bless (+) you, the Father and the Son
and the Holy Spirit.

All   Amen.

6. Recessional Hymn

(B) - IN THE CEMETERY

PC   Since it has pleased Almighty God to call back our brother/
sister from this life to himself, we commit his/her body to
the earth, that it may return to that from which it was made.
Christ was the first to rise from the dead and he will remake
our imperfect bodies to be like his which is now in glory.
Let us entrust our brother/sister to the Lord that he may
raise him/her again at the last day and make him/her one with
his saints in his kingdom.
Let us pray for our brother/sister, pray to Jesus Christ who
has said: "I am the resurrection and the life: whoever believes in me, even though he die, shall live; and every living person who believes in me shall never die but possess
life everlasting."

PC   You wept for Lazarus when he was dead. That you will give us
courage and wipe away the tears from our eyes, Lord Jesus, we
humbly pray:

All   Lord, hear our prayer.

PC   You raised the dead to life; give then eternal life to our
brother/sister, we humbly pray:

All   Lord, hear our prayer.

PC   You promised Paradise to the repentant thief; take then our
brother/sister into eternal happiness, we humbly pray:

All   Lord, hear our prayer.

PC   To our brother/sister, washed in the waters of Baptism and
signed with the oil of salvation, grant a place with your
saints, we humbly pray:

All   Lord, hear our prayer.

PC	To our brother/sister who was nourished at the Sacred Banquet of your Body and Blood, grant a place at the table of your heavenly kingdom, we humbly pray:
All	Lord, hear our prayer.

PC	Bring comfort to us in our sorrow at the loss of our brother/sister. May the faith which is our greatest treasure be our consolation and eternal life our hope, we humbly pray:
All	Lord, hear our prayer.

PC	Let us now pray together as our Lord has taught us to pray:
All	Our Father, who are in heaven.....

PC	We beg you, Lord, to show this mercy to your servant who is now at rest. Make him/her not to suffer for the wrong he/she may have done, for his/her desire was always to do your will. As the true faith was the bond that united him/her to your faithful followers here on earth, so may your mercy hereafter give him/her a place among the saints: Through Jesus Christ your Son, our Lord, who lives and reigns with you in the unity of the Holy Spirit, God, for ever and ever.
All	Amen.

PC	Eternal rest grant unto him/her, O Lord;
All	And let perpetual light shine upon him/her.

PC	Farewell, brother/sister, and pray for us until we are together again (+).

The arrangement of these elements from the ICEL experimental funeral liturgy was the work of Peter E. Fink, S.J.

A MARIAN LITURGY

from three Marian Liturgies arranged by J. J. Kaufmann;
combined by R. F. Hoey, S.J.

ENTRANCE VERSE: (1)

All   (Antiphon) Hail Mary, full of grace.

Lc   The angel of the Lord declared to Mary,
         and she conceived of the Holy Spirit.........All: (Antiphon)
      Behold the handmaid of the Lord,
         be it done to me according to your word......All: (Antiphon)
      The Word was made flesh,
         and dwelt among us.........................All: (Antiphon)

Lc   Pray for us, holy Mother of God.
All   That we may be made worthy of the promises of Christ.

    GLORY TO GOD: (cf. "Hymns of Praise," pp. 14-16.)

    ENTRANCE PRAYER: (2)

PC   United with Mother Church, may we be true, beloved and faith-
      ful disciples and true brothers of Jesus, like the beloved
      disciple who became the son of Mary.
      Like him who received Mary his mother into his own home, may
      we receive the Church our mother into our lives, like true
      sons of the Father and true brothers of Jesus.
All   Amen.

    FIRST READING: 1 Cor. 7:25-34.

    GRADUAL; ALLELUIA: (3)

All   Hail Mary, full of grace,
      the Lord is with you.
      Blessed are you among women
      and blessed is the fruit
      of your womb, Jesus, our Brother.
         Alleluia. Alleluia.
      The important thing about Mary
      is that her Son turned out so well. Alleluia.

    SECOND READING: Lk. 1:26-55.

    CREED: (4)

All   We believe in the only God who is creator of all things and
             is Father,
         in his eternally-begotten Son who is our Lord Jesus
             Christ.

- 160 -

and in the Holy Spirit who proceeds from the Father and
    the Son as their eternal love.
We believe that Mary is the mother, who remained ever a
    virgin, of our God and Saviour Jesus Christ.
We believe in original sin and that Christ redeemed us from
    this and all personal sins.
We believe in the holiness, universality, and apostolicity
    of the Church,
    that it is indefectibly one in faith,
    and that the celebration of the Eucharist is the sacri-
    fice of Calvary rendered sacramentally present.
We confess that the kingdom of God is not of this world
    whose form is passing.
    and that it consists of an ever more ardent response to
    the love of God.
We believe in the life eternal, in the communion of all the
    faithful in Christ.
Blessed be God! Amen.

OFFERTORY SONG: (5)

Mary the dawn,
  Christ the perfect day;
Mary the gate,
  Christ the heavenly way.
Mary the root,
  Christ the mystic vine;
Mary the wheat-sheaf,
  Christ the living bread.
Mary the Temple,
  Christ the Temple's Lord;

Mary the shrine,
  Christ the God adored.
Mary the beacon,
  Christ the haven's rest;
Mary the mirror,
  Christ the vision blest.
Mary the mother,
  Christ the mother's Son;
both ever blest
  while endless ages run.

OFFERTORY VERSE: Jn. 2:2-5 (TJB).

All   When they ran out of wine,
      since the wine provided for the
          wedding was all finished,
      the mother of Jesus said to him,
      "They have no wine."
      Jesus said, "Woman, why turn to me?
      My hour has not come yet."
      His mother said to the servants,
      "Do whatever he tells you."

EUCHARISTIC PRAYER: (cf. ##601-636, pp. 34-115.)

THE LORD'S PRAYER: Mt. 6:9-13 (TJB).

All   Our Father in heaven,
      may your name be held holy,
      your kingdom come,
      your will be done,

on earth as in heaven.
Give us this day our daily bread.
And forgive us our debts,
as we have forgiven those who are in debt to us.
And do not put us to the test,
but save us from the evil one.

COMMUNION HYMN: [6]

All   Blessed are you, Mary: in you the prophecies are fulfilled
and the dark sayings of the prophets explained.
Moses foretold you by the burning bush and the cloud,
Jacob by the ladder leading to heaven,
David by the ark of the covenant,
Ezechiel by the door that was closed and sealed.
And now in your birth their mysterious words are made plain.
Glory to the Father who sent his only Son to manifest
    himself through Mary,
to free us from error and make her memory glorious in heaven
    and on earth.

COMMUNION PRAYER: [7]

PC   Mary, teach me the true meaning of compassion. Show me what
lies beyond the emotion of human pity, and lead me to that
supernatural view of natural suffering which invites my active and Godward cooperation.
Let me come out from the shelter of my life, and meet the
miseries of your Son's Mystical Body in the spirit with which
you went out to meet your Son.
All   Amen.

LITURGICAL SOURCES:

(1)   A combined adaptation of the "Hail Mary" and the "Angelus"
by the arranger.
(2)   Adapted from Mary, Mother of All Christians, by Max Thurian,
New York: Herder and Herder, 1964, p. 166.
(3)   "our Brother" added to "Hail Mary" by arranger;
(Alleluia verse): Sr. Corita Kent, I.H.M.: Newsweek; December 25,
1967, p. 48. (Alleluias added by arranger.)
(4)   Pope Paul VI, in National Catholic Reporter; July 10, 1968,
p. 7 (adapted by arranger).
(5)   Anonymous.
(6)   Balai - fifth century, from Early Christian Prayers; ed. A.
Hamman; Chicago: Henry Regnery Co., 1961, p. 188.
(7)   The Way of the Cross, by Hubert Van Zeller, O.S.B.: Springfield, Ill.: Templegate Publishers, 1958, Fourth Station.

MASS OF CHRIST THE SERVANT

John C. L'Heureux, S.J.

Introduction

This Mass was written for the Chapel of Christ the Servant at
Cranwell School in Lenox, Massachusetts. The Proper will be submitted to Rome for approval. The Offertory (cf. #5), Preface and
Canon (cf. #6) are included in this draft merely because they are
more in accord with the language and intent of the readings and
prayers of the Mass they accompany. The accompanying Prayer of
the Faithful is included as a suggestion.

All texts for the Mass are taken from The Jerusalem Bible (Lon-
don, 1966); the translations are almost invariably superior in
quality to any others available and, important for the liturgy,
they lend themselves particularly well to oral reading.

As to the Offertory, Preface and Canon. The Offertory is
clearly a free translation and an extensive simplification of the
present Roman Offertory. The Preface is altogether original, an
attempt at a simple and inclusive hymn of praise and thanksgiving
after the manner of early Christian prayers. The Canon draws
freely on all existent Canons though it takes its structural outline from the present Roman Canon (Eucharistic Prayer I). This
was quite deliberate, a way of preserving a feeling of continuity
for those who feel that the "old Mass" is the only Mass and a
rather pleasing way of including Bishop, Pope, Christians, unbelievers, etc. in the Canon itself, though strictly speaking they
belong - along with the Blessed Virgin and the Saints - in the
Liturgy of the Word. The content of the Canon, it seems to me,
should be at once solidly theological and readily comprehensible;
too often in the Roman Canon the former has been sought at the ex-
pense of the latter. The Offertory, Preface and Canon have been
tried at some length in privately conducted experimental Masses;
this final redaction has seemed the most suitable.

I have tried to make all decisions in the light of Vatican II's
statement on the reform of the liturgy: "both texts and rites
should be drawn up so that they express more clearly the holy
things which they signify. Christian people, as far as possible,
should be able to understand them with ease and to take part in
them fully, actively, and as befits a community." (Constitution
on the Liturgy, III, 21.)

And so, the Mass:

Entrance Hymn: 1 Jn. 4:20-21.

All   Anyone who says, "I love God,"
       and hates his brother,
       is a liar,
       since a man who does not love the brother that he can see
       cannot love God, whom he has never seen.
       So this is the commandment that he has given us,
       that anyone who loves God must also love his brother.

       Glory be to the Father and to the Son and to the Holy Spirit
       as it was in the beginning, is now, and ever shall be,
       world without end. Amen.

       Anyone who says, "I love God,"
       and hates his brother,
       is a liar,
       since a man who does not love the brother that he can see
       cannot love God, whom he has never seen.

Entrance Prayer:

PC   Father, your Son has told us that we cannot love him unless
       we also love our brother, that we cannot serve him unless we
       also serve our brother. We ask you now for a deeper under-
       standing of his words.
       Through Jesus Christ your Son, our Lord, who lives and reigns
       with you in the unity of the Holy Spirit, God, forever and
       ever.
All   Amen.

First Reading: 1 Jn. 3:11-18 (TJB, N.T., p. 415).

Meditation Hymn: Mt. 25:40, 45.

All   "I tell you solemnly, in so far as you did this to one of
       the least of these brothers of mine, you did it to me."
       "I tell you solemnly, in so far as you neglected to do this
       to one of the least of these, you neglected to do it to me."

Second Reading: Mk. 10:35-45 (TJB, N.T., pp. 79-80).

Homily

Creed

Prayer of the Faithful:

PC   That the holy Church of God, both the hierarchy and the wit-
       nessing faithful, become increasingly aware of her function
       as servant: let us pray to the Lord;
All   Lord, hear our prayer.

- 164 -

PC   That among nations there may be peace and justice which is founded on respect for human dignity within all races, creeds, and colors: let us pray to the Lord;

All   Lord, hear our prayer.

PC   That Christian families may so love one another that the presence of Christ will be manifest among them always: let us pray to the Lord;

All   Lord, hear our prayer.

PC   That married couples find their vocation in being living witnesses to the love of Christ for his Church: let us pray to the Lord;

All   Lord, hear our prayer.

PC   That there be such unity in the Church that all men may know that the Father has sent his Son Jesus Christ who truly dwells among us: let us pray to the Lord;

All   Lord, hear our prayer.

PC   Let us pray: Almighty Father, your Son has told us that whatever we ask in his name will be granted us; we ask you to make us one in the bonds of fraternal love and to make us other Christs in the service of our brothers. This we ask through your Son Jesus Christ, who lives and reigns with you in the unity of the Holy Spirit, God, forever and ever.

All   Amen.

Offertory Hymn: Mt. 10:40, 42.

All   "Anyone who welcomes you welcomes me, and those who welcome me welcome the one who sent me."
      "If anyone gives so much as a cup of cold water to one of these little ones because he is a disciple, then I tell you solemnly, he will most certainly not lose his reward."

Offertory: cf. #505, p. 24.

Summary Prayer Over the Gifts:

PC   Lord Jesus Christ, this sacrifice we celebrate reveals your perfect service of the Father and your overwhelming love for us. Unite our offering of self with yours; unite us now with one another. You who live and reign with God the Father in the unity of the Holy Spirit, God, forever and ever.

All   Amen.

Preface and Canon: cf. #629, p. 97.

("The Lord's Prayer" may be recited while Communion is distributed, and the "Gloria" when the last of the wine has been consumed.)

Communion Hymn: Lk. 22:26-27.

All   The greatest among you must behave as if he were the young-
est, the leader as if he were the one who serves. For which
is the greater: the one at table or the one who serves? The
one at table, surely? Yet here I am among you as one who
serves!

Prayer After Communion:

PC   Father, we who have received the Body and Blood of your Son,
Jesus Christ, ask that we be open to his coming in whatever
way he wishes to enter our lives, prompt always to listen to
his Holy Spirit. Through Jesus Christ your Son, our Lord,
who lives and reigns with you in the unity of the Holy Spirit,
God, forever and ever.

All   Amen.

MASS OF CHRISTIAN BROTHERHOOD

Arranged by Patrick McShane, adapted by R. F. Hoey, S.J.

ENTRANCE RITE: Ps. 118:1-4, 8 (CCD)

All   Happy are they whose way is blameless,
        who walk in the law of the Lord.
    Happy are they who observe his decrees,
        who seek him with all their heart,
    And do no wrong,
        but walk in his ways.

    You have commanded that your precepts be diligently kept.
        I will keep your statutes; do not utterly forsake me.

    Glory be to the Father.....etc...... (Repeat: Happy - ways)

PRAYER OF THE ASSEMBLY: 1 Jn. 4:15-16 (TJB)

PC   Let us pray:
    if anyone acknowledges that Jesus is the Son of God,
    God lives in him, and he in God.
    We ourselves have known and put our faith in
    God's love towards ourselves.
    God is love
    and anyone who lives in love lives in God,
    and God lives in him.
        Teach us, God, to realize the meaning of these words.
    Through Jesus Christ, your Son, our Lord, who lives and
    reigns with you in the unity of the Holy Spirit, God,
    forever and ever.

All   Amen.

FIRST READING: Col. 3:12-15.

MEDITATION VERSE: 1 Jn. 4:20-21 (TJB).
ALLELUIA VERSE: Ps. 139:14 (TJB).

All   Anyone who says, "I love God,"
    and hates his brother,
    is a liar,
    since a man who does not love the brother that he can see
    cannot love God, whom he has never seen.
    So this is the commandment that he has given us,
    that anyone who loves God must also love his brother.

    Alleluia, Alleluia. I thank you:
    for the wonder of myself, for the wonder of your works.
    Alleluia.

OFFERTORY VERSE: Mt. 5:23-24 (TJB).

All   If you are bringing your offering to the altar and there remember that your brother has something against you, leave your offering there before the altar, go and be reconciled with your brother first, and then come back and present your offering.

PRAYER OVER THE GIFTS:

PC   O God, your Son tells us that we must love one another. Teach us, Father, by this offering we have made to you with our brothers here, to put on love. This we ask of you through Jesus Christ, your Son, our Lord, who lives and reigns with you in the unity of the Holy Spirit, one God, for ever and ever.

All   Amen.

COMMUNION PRAYER: (to take the place of a hymn) Malcolm
    Boyd: "Are You Running with Me, Jesus?", p. 33.

All   Because it is for this that you were called together as part of one body. Always be thankful.

Lc   I've searched for community in many places, Jesus. I was often looking in the wrong places, but I don't think my motive was altogether wrong. I was looking futilely and hopelessly there for fellowship, belonging, and acceptance. Now, in this moment, which many people would label "loneliness," or "nothingness," I want to thank you, Jesus. In this moment...in this place and with these other persons...I have found community where and as it is. It seems to me it is your gift. I am here with these others for only a few hours. I will not be with them tomorrow. But I won't be searching so desperately anymore. I know I must accept community where you offer it to me. I accept it at this moment. Thank you, Jesus.

All   Because it is for this that you were called together as part of one body. Always be thankful.

PRAYER AFTER COMMUNION:

PC   Let us pray:
Father, it is with great joy that we bring to a close this Eucharistic Meal, joining in praise with our brothers. It was possible only because you saw that what you have created is good. We ask you to keep the peace of Christ, your Son, in our hearts. This we ask of you through Jesus Christ, your Son, our Lord, who lives and reigns with you in the unity of the Holy Spirit, one God, for ever and ever.

All   Amen.

A THANKSGIVING LITURGY

F. Michael Perko, S.J., and John S. Chapman, S.J.

Commentary: See end of Liturgy.

ENTRANCE RITE

General Confession:

PC   In the name of the Father, and of the Son, and of the Holy Spirit. Amen.
Let us acknowledge our ingratitude before the Father, and in the words of the Prodigal son say: Father, we have sinned against heaven and before you; we no longer deserve to be called your sons.
I will go to the altar of God.

All   To God who gives joy to my youth.

PC   Our help is in the name of the Lord.

All   Who made heaven and earth.

PC   We confess...

All   ...to Almighty God, to Blessed Mary.....etc.....

PC   May the Almighty and Merciful God grant us pardon, absolution, and remission of all our sins.

All   Amen.

Entrance Song: suggestions:
> "Sing To God A Brand New Canticle" by Paul Quinlan, S.J.
> "For Evermore" by Ray Repp

Glory To God

LITURGY OF THE WORD

Entrance Prayer:

PC   The Lord be with you.

All   And with you.

PC   Let us pray: O Lord, we are united here today to worship you in praise and thanksgiving. May these dispositions make our hearts rich soil into which you can plant your word and make it grow. We ask you this through Jesus Christ, your Son, our Lord, who lives with you in the unity of the Holy Spirit for ever and ever.

All   Amen.

First Reading: from History of the Pilgrim Colony by William Bradford (cf. end of Liturgy; or Deut. 26:1-11).

Scriptural Response: Lk. 1:46b-55, "The Magnificat"; may be postponed for "meditative reading" after Gospel; may be recited by all or sung or read by one person.

Gospel: Lk. 8:4-8.

Homily, Dialogue Homily, Time of Silence, or "The Magnificat"

Prayer of the Faithful:

PC   The Lord be with you.
All   And with you.
PC   Let us pray: We acknowledge the gifts you have given us
       through our country, Lord, and we bless you for them. Yet we
       remember that as we have greatly received, so in the same
       measure are we responsible. Forbid that we should be unfaith-
       ful to our task, or that the fire which has been passed on to
       a new generation of Americans, to us, should perish.
       Help us to be worthy of our fathers, and of our fathers' God:
All   Help us, O God, to be faithful.

PC   To all the high desires of the pioneers and prophets:
All   Help us, O God, to be faithful.

PC   To their belief in the possibilities of common men:
All   Help us, O God, to be faithful.

PC   To their passion for freedom and their readiness to die in its
       defense:
All   Help us, O God, to be faithful.

PC   To their scorn of tyranny, and their trust in men to rule
       themselves:
All   Help us, O God, to be faithful.

PC   To their vision of a human commonwealth in which the people of
       many lands may share:
All   Help us, O God, to be faithful.

PC   To their release from the passion and prejudice of an old
       world and their will to build a new:
All   Help us, O God, to be faithful.

PC   O God, our fathers trusted in you, and you delivered them.
All   Help us, O God, to be faithful.

PC   So, we ask you, Lord God, to strengthen us, and to lead us on
       the path of righteousness.   Through Jesus Christ, our Lord.
All   Amen.

LITURGY OF THE EUCHARIST

Offering of the Gifts: cf. ##501-507; pp. 23-25; or:
                        Deut. 26:1-11, read as follows:
Commentator (as community places hosts on paten): vv. 1-3;

- 170 -

<u>Commentator</u> (as the paten and the water and wine are accepted
                by the priest): vv. 4-5a;
<u>PC or All</u> (as the priest offers the gifts): vv. 5b-10a;
<u>Commentator</u> - vv. 10b-11.

Prayer Over the Gifts:

PC   Let us pray: Lord, please accept these gifts we offer you today in thanksgiving for your love of us which has shown itself
in countless ways. Accept them and bless them that they may
become the body of your Son and symbols of our redemption.
Through Jesus Christ your Son, our Lord, who lives and reigns
with you in the unity of the Holy Spirit, God, forever and
ever.

All   Amen.

Preface

PC   The Lord be with you.
All   And with your spirit.
PC   Lift up your hearts.
All   We have lifted them up to the Lord.
PC   Let us give thanks to the Lord our God.
All   It is right and just.

PC   It is most fitting that we always and everywhere give thanks
to you, Holy Father, Almighty and Eternal God. Today especially we thank you for our country, beautiful and free, a land
of opportunity and hope.
For sunshine, blue skies, lakes and mountain streams;
for the herds in the pasture, and the fields ready for harvest:
All   We thank you, Lord.

PC   For children's smiles and the vision of youth;
for the love in parents' eyes:
All   We thank you, Lord.

PC   For great men of genius who work wonders in our behalf:
All   We thank you, Lord.

PC   For all the men and women who work unnoticed yet who give our
country its strength:
All   We thank you, Lord.

PC   For the public servants and military men who give their lives
for us:
All   We thank you, Lord.

PC   Yes, Father, we thank you for all your wonderful gifts, too
many to number. In praise we join our hearts and voices and
joyfully sing:
All   Holy, holy, holy.....

Eucharistic Prayer: Anaphora of St. Hippolytus; #602, p. 34.

The Lord's Prayer:

PC   Let us pray: United here as your children, thankfully we
        pray to you as Our Father, saying in the words of Christ...
All   Our Father.....etc.....

PC   Deliver us, we beg you, O Lord, from every evil, past, pres-
        ent, and to come; and through the intercession of all the
        saints grant peace in our days, that with thankful hearts we
        may praise you who deliver us from all sin.   Through Jesus
        Christ your Son, our Lord, who lives and reigns with you in
        the unity of the Holy Spirit, God, for ever and ever.
All   Amen.

Ceremony of Peace:

PC   Lord Jesus Christ, who said to your apostles: "Peace I leave
        you, my peace I give you," look not upon our sins, but upon
        our faith.   Be pleased to give us, your Church gathered here,
        peace and unity in accordance with your will.   You who live
        and reign God, for ever and ever.
All   Amen.

PC   (breaking the host, he puts a piece in the chalice, and then
        turns to those near him saying:)
        May the peace of the Lord be always with you.
All   And with you.
        (Now each extends the greeting of peace to those around him.)

Communion:

PC   (before receiving the Body of Christ:)
        "See the days are coming--it is the Lord who speaks--when I
        will establish a new covenant with the House of Israel and
        the House of Judah, but not a covenant like the one I made
        with their ancestors on the day I took them by the hand to
        bring them out of the land of Egypt.   They broke that cove-
        nant of mine.   No, this is the covenant I will make with the
        House of Israel when those days arrive.   I will put my law
        into their minds, and write it on their hearts.   Then I will
        be their God and they shall be my people." (Heb. 8:7) (TJB).
        The Body of Christ.
All   Amen.

PC   (before receiving the Chalice:)
        What return shall we make to the Lord for all he has done for
        us?   We shall take the chalice of salvation and call on the
        name of the Lord.
        The Blood of Christ.
All   Amen.

Thanksgiving: Say or sing Ps. 92, or Ps. 96, or Ps. 138.

PC   The Lord be with you.
All   And with you.
PC   Let us pray: O Lord, we have sounded our thanksgiving to you;
         now, filled through Communion with your Son, help us to live
         what we have said.   Through Jesus Christ...
All   Amen.

Blessing and Dismissal

_____

Commentary for the Liturgy

Before entrance prayers: We celebrate today in the tradition
of America the day of Great Thanksgiving to God for our land.

     As citizens of the United States,
we have been brought into a land flowing with milk and honey.
We live in a land of science fiction. We have opportunities at
the touch of a dial that William Bradford, the head of the Plymouth Colony, could never have envisioned.
     And so now, we who follow these Pilgrims seem to go to a wed-
ding feast which they have prepared for us.

     As citizens of the Kingdom of Christ,
we have been brought into a land flowing with grace and love.
We live in a land of new redemption. We have opportunities coming
from the touch of Christ that Abraham, Moses, and Isaiah could
only envision.
     And so now, we who follow Christ go to a Eucharistic Feast
which he has prepared for us.

     Today is a joyful day! Our first act of joy is an act of sor-
row. Our deepest joy is that Christ came to call sinners to life.
As ungrateful as the Prodigal Son, we go to our Father not worthy
to be called his sons; and he will celebrate our return with a
Feast.
     Today is a joyful day! We can sing to God a new song with all
our heart.

     Before Readings: Our second act of joy is to listen to the
Word of God. We hear the account of (the Plymouth Colony's strug-
gles to establish our land of freedom. Then we hear of) God's
bringing the Hebrews into their Land of Freedom.
     Our land of freedom begins with Mary's "Magnificat" and grows
with our understanding of Christ's Parable of the Sower.

     Before the Offertory: Our next act of joy is to bring our
gifts. The Hebrews brought gifts to Yahweh in thanksgiving for
his saving act, for Yahweh brought them out of the land

of Egypt into a new Land of Promise. We offer our gifts to God in thanksgiving for his act in Jesus Christ who brings us into the land of promise, the Kingdom of God.

Before the Eucharistic Prayer: Our greatest act of joy and thanksgiving is the proclaiming of the saving act of Jesus Christ through his meal.

First Reading: from History of the Pilgrim Colony, by William Bradford:

"...And the pilgrims were only to rest on God's providence; many times at night not knowing where to have a bit of anything to eat the next day, and so, as one well observed, they had need to pray that God would give them their Daily Bread--above all people in the world. Yet they bore these wants with great patience, and alacrity of spirit; with their miseries they opened a way to these new lands; and after these storms, with what ease other men came to inhabit in them in respect of the calamities these men suffered: so as they seem to go to a bride's feast where all things are prepared for them."

THE EUCHARISTIC LITURGY

As prepared by the people of St. Mark's In-The-Bowery for use in special ecumenical occasions when men meet for the first and the last time.

THE PREPARATION

(At the appointed time, when all the people have assembled, the bishop, as president of the assembly, or some presbyter appointed to stand in his place, facing the assembly, shall say:)

PC   We are here.
All   In the name of Jesus Christ.

PC,All   We are here because we are men - but we deny our
         humanity. We are stubborn fools and liars to ourselves.
         We do not love others. We war against life. We hurt
         each other. We are sorry for it and know we are sick
         from it. We seek new life.

PC   Giver of life, heal us and free us to be men.

PC,All   Holy Spirit, speak to us. Help us to listen, for we are
         very deaf. Come, fill this moment.

         (Silence for a time.)

THE SERVICE OF THE WORD

Old Testament

Psalm (said responsively)

Epistle (read from the same place and in like manner to Old
         Testament lesson)

Hymn

Gospel (read in the midst of the assembly, all the people
         facing the reader)

Sermon

Intercessions (the deacon shall bid the prayers and interces-
         sions of the assembly. He may lead them in a litany or with
         free prayers.)

THE OFFERTORY

PC   "If you are offering your gift at the altar, and there remember
      that your brother has something against you, leave your gift

at the altar and go; first be reconciled to your brother, and then come and offer your gift." (Mt. 5:23.)

(After which he will turn to the deacon first and then the reader saying:)

PC   Peace, my friend.
(and the deacon will answer:)
CC   Peace.

(Then the deacon and the reader will give the "Peace" to representatives of the congregation gathered before the altar table, and they in turn will pass it to all the people, while others will collect the alms.)

PC   I appeal to you therefore, brethren, by the mercies of God, to present your bodies as a living sacrifice, holy and acceptable to God, which is your spiritual worship. Do not be conformed to this world, but be transformed by the renewal of your mind, that you may prove what is the will of God, what is good and acceptable and perfect. (Rom. 12:1-2.)

(Then shall be sung a hymn, during which time representatives of the people will bring the money along with the bread, water and wine, and place them on the holy table. The deacon shall prepare the bread and wine.)

THE ACT OF THANKSGIVING

PC   Lift up your hearts.
All We lift them to the Lord.
PC   Let us give thanks for God's glory.
All We give thanks; we rejoice in the glory of all creation.

PC   All glory be to you, O Father, who sent your only son into the world to be a man, born of a woman's womb, to die for us on a cross that was made by us.

All He came for us. Help us to accept his coming.

PC   He walked among us, a man, on our earth, in our world of conflict, and commanded us to remember his death, his death which gives us life; and to wait for him until he comes again in glory.

All We remember his death; we live by his presence; we wait for his coming.

PC   (Lifting up the bread in thanksgiving:) On the night he was betrayed, the Lord Jesus took bread, he gave thanks; he broke it, and gave it to his disciples, saying, "Take, eat; this is my body. Do this in remembrance of me."

(Lifting up the wine in thanksgiving:) He also took the cup; he gave thanks; and gave it to them, saying, "Drink of it, all of you; this is my blood of the covenant, which is poured out for many for the forgiveness of sins."

All   Come, Lord Jesus, come.

PC   Therefore, remembering his death, believing in his rising from the grave, longing to recognize his presence; now, in this place, we obey his command; we offer bread and wine, we offer ourselves, to be used.

All   Everything is yours, O Lord; we return the gift which first you gave us.

PC   (May extend his hands over the bread and wine:) Accept it, Father. Send down the spirit of life and power, glory and love, upon these people, upon this bread and wine, that to us they may be his body and his blood.

All   Come, risen Lord, live in us that we may live in you.

PC   Now with all men who ever were, are, and will be, with all creation in all time, with joy we sing.

PC,All   Holy, holy, holy, Lord God almighty, all space and all time show forth your glory now and always. Amen.

PC   And now, in his words, we are bold to say:
All   "The Lord's Prayer"

PC   (Breaks the bread before the assembly, saying:)
        The gifts of God for the people of God.
All   Amen.

THE COMMUNION

(Then shall the president and other ministers receive Holy Communion into their hands, and then distribute the bread and wine to all present.)

PC   The body of Christ.   PC   The blood of Christ.
All   Amen.   All   Amen.

(When all have communicated, the president and other ministers shall gather and consume the fragments, while a hymn is sung.)

THE DISMISSAL

PC   Go. Serve the Lord. You are free.
All   Amen.

....

THE SACRAMENT OF RECONCILIATION

THE SACRAMENT OF RECONCILIATION

James K. Serrick, S.J.

I

Entrance Hymn (melody of O Sacred Head Now Wounded)

O God, all-knowing Father, most merciful and kind;
We humbly trust your patience, that mercy we may find;
As sinful, erring members, Christ's body we have harmed
Thus disregarding wholly our Master's law of love.

O Lord, you know our weakness, brought on by Adam's fall;
And in your gentle meekness, You heed the sinner's call.
Look down in loving kindness, upon our saddened plight;
Then heal our stubborn blindness, and give us, Lord, your light.

Opening Prayer (kneel) - cf. #214, p. 11.

First Reading: Daniel, 9:4-17 (sit).

Reader: Together with the prophet, Daniel, let us take our place
in the ranks of sinful mankind and plead with the Lord for forgiveness.

Meditative Response: Daniel, 9:17-19 (all).

Second Reading: Matthew, 9:1-8 (stand).

Reader: God sent his only Son to save us from our own weakness
and the powers of evil. Let us be mindful of the presence of
Jesus among us as we hear how he dealt with the paralytic at
Capharnaum.

Response

All   O Lord Jesus Christ, you forgave the sins of the paralytic
      because of his great faith in you.
      Give us a genuine faith in your power and willingness
          to forgive our sins.
      Let us too arise and walk in the strength of your grace
      and the support of your loving friendship.
      All praise to your heavenly Father who has seen fit to give
          such power to men.

Third Reading: Matthew, 9:9-13.

Reader: Jesus calls all men to personal union with himself. His
call goes forth especially to those who consider themselves un-

worthy of his sacred presence. Let us listen to the call of
Matthew the apostle.

Response

All   O Lord Jesus Christ, we give you thanks that you have come
           to call us sinners.
       You forgive our guilt and desire to be our companion at the
           banquet table of the Eucharist.
       For it is in the breaking of the bread that we recognize you
           in our presence.
       It is in the drinking of the cup of your blood
           poured out for the forgiveness of sins
       that we find reconciliation with you and with our brothers.

Litany for Pardon (kneel)

(melody)

Hear, O Lord, and grant pardon.

PC   If we say we have no <u>sin</u>, we deceive ourselves and the truth /
       is <u>not in</u> us. (1 Jn. <u>1</u>:8.)
All   Hear, O Lord, and grant pardon.

PC   With Peter the apostle we <u>say</u>: "Depart from me, Lord, for I /
       am a <u>sinful</u> man.
All   Hear, O Lord, and grant pardon.

PC   Mindful of Mary Magdalen, Peter, and the thief on the <u>cross</u>,
          we come to /
       you in <u>confidence</u>.
All   Hear, O Lord, and grant pardon.

PC   You, O Christ, remain our advocate to plead our cause be- /
       fore <u>the Father</u>. (1 Jn. 2:1.)
All   Hear, O Lord, and grant pardon.

PC   Not those in <u>health</u>, but the sick have need of /
       a <u>physician</u>. (Lk. 5:31.)
All   Hear, O Lord, and grant pardon.

PC   You, O Lord, the Most Holy, have taken our sins upon <u>yourself</u>;
          in your body you bore them on the /
       <u>wood</u> of the cross. (1 Pet. 2:24.)
All   Hear, O Lord, and grant pardon.

Collective Prayer (stand)

PC   The Lord be with you.   All And with your spirit.
PC   Let us pray in silence. (Pause for reflection.)

PC   O God, you desire the repentance of the sinner and not his
      death. Take into consideration our frail human nature. Be
      merciful to us for we know that we are dust and to dust we
      shall return because of our sinfulness. Forgive us and grant
      us the rewards you have promised to sincere penitents.
      Through Christ our Lord.
All   Amen.

Calling Forth of the Penitents

Deacon or Reader: Dear brothers in Christ, we are all guilty be-
for the pure and holy God. But in his mercy God has given to his
Church, to his holy People, the sacrament of reconciliation. For
our brothers who are about to partake in this holy sacrament we
beg the grace of humility, of sincerity and true sorrow. Let us
pray for them that God may sanctify them and make them one with us
through the bond of his grace. The penitents will now step forth.

     (Those who wish to receive the sacrament come to the
     middle aisle and the celebrant leads them to the back
     of the chapel. The celebrant enters the confessional
     and hears each one individually. Afterwards they kneel
     in the back of the chapel.)

     (While the penitents go to the back of the chapel to
     receive the sacrament, the others kneel and recite Ps. 50.)

     (All should spend the time in meditation until the
     penitents are ready to rejoin the community. As the
     celebrant leads them up the aisle, all stand and sing
     the refrain: "We shall go up with joy to the house of
     our God.")

     (When all are in their places, the singing is ended
     and all sit.)

Admonition of the Deacon (or Celebrant)

   Dear brothers in Christ, when any man sins or commits a fault,
he is guilty before the Lord and must ask pardon of God for his
offense. At the same time, he offends against his fellow Christians and must ask pardon of the Christian community as a whole or
through the one appointed to represent that community. The Lord
has told us first to be reconciled with one another and only then
to approach the banquet table of the Eucharist. The grace of Christ
binds us together in a single body. One man's good contributes to
the good of all and builds up the body to the full stature intended by God. One man's deficiency, on the other hand, weakens the
whole body and causes all the members to suffer. The stronger
members must come to the aid of the weaker by prayer, penance, and
good example. Those who have offended must give an example of

humility and sincere contrition by admitting their failings and proving their words by accepting the penance imposed and making a real effort not to repeat their sin or fault. All those in the community who have a fault to confess will rise and, in the true humility of a follower of Jesus, state their faults openly. Those who listen are admonished in the Lord to remember their own faults and failings, to accept their brethren as they are, and to pray for the unity and strengthening of the whole Christian community.

> (Those who are to accuse themselves rise and state their faults. At the end, one delegated asks pardon for faults not mentioned by others.)

Petition of the Deacon (or Reader)

Reverend Father, you have heard the public and private confessions of some of our brethren present. In their name I beg you to impose a penance on all who have spoken with faith and open sincerity.

The Penance

PC   For all who have received the sacrament, besides any penance imposed privately, your penance will be to recite Psalm 31. For those who have admitted their faults publicly to the community, the penance will be to recite Psalm 31 and to perform some freely chosen act of charity that will contribute to the good of the community. All present, moreover, are invited to share the penance with those upon whom it is imposed and to pray for their perseverance and spiritual improvement in the Lord.

> (All kneel and recite Psalm 31.)

Declaration of Forgiveness

PC   Our help is in the name of the Lord
All   Who made heaven and earth.
PC   Save your servants.
All   Who trust in you, my God.
PC   Let the enemy have no power over them.
All   And let not the son of evil dare to harm them.
PC   Be a tower of strength for them, O Lord.
All   Against the attack of the enemy.
PC   O Lord, hear my prayer.
All   And let my cry come to you.
PC   The Lord be with you.
All   And with your spirit.

PC   Let us pray: O God, to whom it belongs always to show mercy and to spare, receive our prayer that these your servants who have admitted their sinfulness before you and the whole court of heaven and before their brethren may be pardoned by your mercy. Through Christ our Lord.

All   Amen.

PC   May almighty God have mercy on you, forgive your sins, and bring you to life everlasting. May he bring you into the fullness of unity with all your brethren through this sacrament of reconciliation and through partaking in the sacrament of the body and blood of Christ our Lord.

All   Amen.

    (The celebrant kisses the altar and passes the handshake to the deacon. All receive it using the form: "Peace be with you / And with you.")

Concluding Hymn: "Where Charity and Love Prevail"

II

Opening Hymn - as on p. 179.

Opening Prayer - cf. #214, p. 11 (kneel).

Scripture Reading and Homily (stand, then sit)

Response: "Have mercy, Lord, cleanse me from all my sins."

Confessions (names and locations of confessors)

Psalm 31 (by others during confessions)

Individual and Common Chapter of Faults (sit)

    (Those wishing to ask the pardon of all for any failing should do so while remaining seated. Raise your hand slightly to receive the acknowledgment of the celebrant.)

Declaration of Forgiveness (kneel)

    (As on p. 182, from "Our help..." to "...your spirit."

PC   Let us pray to the Lord in silence. (Pause.)

Concluding Orations

Giving of the Handshake of Peace and Friendship (cf. above)

Closing Hymn: "Where Charity and Love Prevail"

Entrance Hymn - as on p. 179.

Opening Prayer (kneel)

All   O God, most merciful Father,
we have come together to confess our sinfulness before you.
You remember that we are dust and you know our weakness.
Have mercy on us, O Lord.
Cleanse us of our sinfulness.
Purify our dedication to your service.
Remove the barriers that divide us, the shortcomings that
     spring from human weakness.
Teach us to forgive and bear with others as you forgive and
     bear with us.
Let our hearts of stone become hearts of flesh
so that there may be no obstacle to our love for you
     and for one another.

Scripture Reading

Response: (from Psalm 50)

All   1 Have mercy on me, O God, according to your steadfast
          love;
          according to your abundant mercy blot out my
          transgressions.
      2 Wash me thoroughly from my iniquity,
          and cleanse me from my sin!
      4 Against you, you only, have I sinned,
          and done that which is evil in your sight,
      8 Fill me with joy and gladness;
          let the bones which you have broken rejoice.
     10 Create in me a clean heart, O God,
          and put a new and right spirit within me.
     11 Cast me not away from your presence,
          and take not your Holy Spirit from me.
     12 Restore to me the joy of your salvation.

      (At this point confessions will be heard privately
      for those who wish to go. At the end of the confession
      the priest will impose a penance and bid you go in peace.
      When confessions have been heard, all re-assemble for
      common absolution.)

Psalm 31

Imposition of Hands
     (part of the sacramental sign)

All   Our blest Redeemer ere he breathed his tender last farewell,
A guide, a comforter bequeathed with us to dwell.

He came his graces to impart, a loving, willing guest;
While he can find one humble heart wherein to rest.

And ev'ry virtue we possess and ev'ry victory won,
And ev'ry thought of holiness are his alone.

(As the priest imposes hands, he says: "May the Holy
Spirit come upon you and forgive your sins.")

Rite of Absolution

PC   Our help is in the name of the Lord.
All Who made heaven and earth.
PC   Save your servants.
All Who trust in you, my God.
PC   O Lord, hear my prayer.
All And let my cry come to you.

PC   May our Lord Jesus Christ absolve you
and by his authority I free you from any obstacle
that hinders your union with God and with the community
of the faithful on earth.
Finally, I absolve you from all your sins
in the name of the Father and of the Son and of the
Holy Spirit.
All Amen.

Concluding Hymn: "They'll Know We Are Christians By Our Love"

....

APPENDIX

THE CONTRIBUTORS

REV. LAWRENCE D. ALBERTSON: Assistant Pastor; St. Agnes Church, Shawnee Mission, Kansas.

REV. JOSEPH A. APPLEYARD, S.J.: Professor of English; Boston College, Chestnut Hill, Massachusetts.

REV. ROBERT A. BAGNATO, S.J.: Professor of Mathematics; Fordham University, Bronx, New York.

WILLIAM BIRMINGHAM: Editor; <u>Cross</u> <u>Currents</u> <u>Quarterly</u> magazine, West Nyack, New York.

REV. MALCOLM BOYD: Episcopalian Chaplain-at-large to American university students.

ROBERT W. CAVANAGH, S.J.: Seminarian; Bellarmine School of Theology, North Aurora, Illinois.

JOHN S. CHAPMAN, S.J.: Seminarian; Bellarmine School of Theology, North Aurora, Illinois.

REV. DAVID L. COOKE, S.J.: Teacher of Theology; Marquette University High School, Milwaukee, Wisconsin.

G. F. COPE: Lecturer, Department of Extra-Mural Studies; University of Birmingham, England.

CLYDE CREWS: Graduate student in Theology; Fordham University, Bronx, New York.

J. G. DAVIES: Professor of Theology; University of Birmingham, England.

REV. FRANCIS DOWLING, S.J.: Theology student; Bellarmine School of Theology, North Aurora, Illinois.

ROBERT R. DWELLEY: Seminarian; Boston College School of Liberal Arts, "Shadowbrook," Lenox, Massachusetts.

REV. JAMES L. EMPEREUR, S.J.: Graduate student in Theology; Pacific School of Religion, Berkeley, California.

REV. ERNEST C. FERLITA, S.J.: Graduate student in Drama; Yale University, New Haven, Connecticut.

PETER E. FINK, S.J.: Seminarian; Woodstock College, Woodstock, Maryland.

REV. DONALD L. GELPI, S.J.: Graduate student in Philosophy; Cambridge, Massachusetts.

REV. FRANCIS GINHAC, S.J.: Dean, Graduate Division of Theology; Fordham University, Bronx, New York.

REV. GEORGE S. GLANZMAN, S.J.: Professor of Theology; Fordham University, Bronx, New York.

REV. BENEDICT J. HABIGER, O.S.B.: Assistant Pastor; St. Joseph's Church, Atchison, Kansas.

REV. LAWRENCE H. JONES, S.J.: Headmaster; Bishop's Latin School, Pittsburgh, Pennsylvania.

J. J. KAUFMANN: Poet-liturgist; Valyermo, California; member of Los Angeles Association of Laymen.

ANNE C. KENNEY: Student; Boston College School of Education, Chestnut Hill, Massachusetts.

REV. J. LEO KLEIN, S.J.: Graduate student in Theology; Fordham University, Bronx, New York.

ROGER P. KUHN: Teacher; Los Angeles, California; Sectional Representative, American Federation of Teachers.

REV. JOHN C. L'HEUREUX, S.J.: Student-writer-poet-liturgist; Cambridge, Massachusetts.

REV. JOHN R. MAY, S.J.: Graduate student in Theology and Literature; Emory University, Atlanta, Georgia.

PATRICK McSHANE: Seminarian; Mt. Angel College Seminary, St. Benedict, Oregon.

ELISABETH A. MEIER: Graduate student in Theology; Fordham University, Bronx, New York.

F. MICHAEL PERKO, S.J.: Seminarian; Boston College School of Philosophy, Weston, Massachusetts.

REV. LOUIS M. SAVARY, S.J.: Author-graduate student in Theology; Catholic University of America, Washington, D.C.

REV. JAMES K. SERRICK, S.J.: Assistant Director of Novices; Colombiere College, Clarkston, Michigan.

REV. FRANCIS W. SWEENEY, S.J.: Professor of English; Boston College, Chestnut Hill, Massachusetts.

REV. JOSEPH A. TETLOW, S.J.: Graduate student in American Studies; Brown University, Providence, Rhode Island.

LEONARD J. TIGHE: Seminarian; St. John's Seminary, Brighton, Massachusetts.

D. A. TYTLER: Director of Religious Education; Anglican Diocese of Birmingham, England.

THE EDITOR

REV. ROBERT F. HOEY, S.J.: former University Chaplain; Boston College, Chestnut Hill, Massachusetts; currently, 1969-70, graduate student in Theology at the University of San Francisco
....

ACKNOWLEDGMENTS

(Listed according to numbered or titled items in this book.)

1) Previously copyrighted material:

Are You Running With Me, Jesus?, by Malcolm Boyd. Copyright (c) 1965, by Malcolm Boyd. Reprinted by permission of the publisher: Holt, Rinehart and Winston, Inc.:
    Mass of Christian Brotherhood.

Baroque Moment, by Francis W. Sweeney, S.J. Copyright (c) 1951, by Declan X. McMullen Co. Reprinted by permission of the author:
    554.

The Book of Common Worship, Provisional Services. The Westminster Press. Copyright (c) 1966, by W. L. Jenkins. Used by permission of the publisher:
    103, 203, 208, 612, 901.

The Book of Common Worship of the Church of South India. Copyright (c), by Oxford University Press. Reprinted with permission of the publisher:
    204, 302, 501.

Copyright (c) 1965, by Malcolm Boyd. Reprinted with permission:
    105.

Confraternity Edition of the Scriptures used with permission of the copyright owner, the Confraternity of Christian Doctrine (Note: excerpts identified by CCD):
    Liturgy of the Liberation of the Soul, Mass of Christian Brotherhood.

Contemporary Liturgy, by John Arthur; copyright (c), Lutheran Student Association. Reprinted with permission of the author:
    101, 404, 504.

The Daily Office, ed. Herbert Lindemann; copyright (c) 1965, Concordia Publishing House. Reprinted with permission of the publisher:
    303.

The Dead Sea Scriptures; copyright (c) 1956, 1964, by Theodor H. Gaster. Reprinted with permission of the publisher, Doubleday & Company, Inc.:
    209.

Early Christian Prayers, ed. A. Hamman. Copyright (c) 1961. Henry Regnery Company. Reprinted with permission of the publisher:
    A Marian Liturgy.

Early Sources of the Liturgy, by Lucien Deiss, C.S.Sp. Translation copyright (c) Geoffrey Chapman, Ltd. Reprinted with permission of Alba House, the American publisher:
    704, 801, 805.

The Eucharistic Liturgy of Taizé, by Max Thurian. (c) 1959 Les Presses de Taizé. This translation (c) The Taizé Community 1962. Reprinted with permission of The Faith Press:
    614.

An <u>Experimental</u> <u>Liturgy</u>, copyright (c) 1958, G. Cope, J. G.
   Davies, D. A. Tytler. Published by the John Knox Press.
   Reprinted with permission of the publisher:
     613.
The <u>Jerusalem</u> <u>Bible</u>, copyright (c) 1966 by Darton, Longmans, &
   Todd, Ltd., and Doubleday & Company, Inc. Used by permission
   of the publishers (Note: excerpts identified by <u>TJB</u>):
     596, 597, 598, 599, 698, 903, 905, 906, 907, 908, 909, 910,
     A Marian Liturgy, Mass of Christ the Servant, Mass of Chris-
     tian Brotherhood, A Thanksgiving Liturgy.
Copyright (c) John L'Heureux, 1967, 1968. All rights reserved.
   Reprinted with permission:
     505, 629, Mass of Christ the Servant.
The <u>Lord's</u> <u>Day</u> <u>Service</u>; copyright (c) 1964, United Church Press.
   Used by permission of the publisher:
     210, 402, 502.
(Adapted from) <u>Mary</u>, <u>Mother</u> <u>of</u> <u>All</u> <u>Christians</u>, by Max Thurian; New
   York: (c) Herder and Herder, 1964; used with permission:
     A Marian Liturgy.
The <u>Mass</u> <u>Reformed</u>, by Roger P. Kuhn. Copyright (c) 1965, by the
   Catholic Action Office, Notre Dame, Indiana. Reprinted with
   permission:
     201, 305, 405, 628.
<u>Revised</u> <u>Standard</u> <u>Version</u> of the Bible. Old Testament, copyright
   (c) 1952, New Testament copyright (c) 1946, by Division of
   Christian Education of the National Council of the Churches of
   Christ in the U. S. A. Reprinted with permission (Note: ex-
   cerpts identified by <u>RSV</u>):
     699, 701, 702, St. Mark's Church Eucharistic Liturgy.
The <u>Way</u> <u>of</u> <u>the</u> <u>Cross</u>, by Hubert Van Zeller, O.S.B.: Springfield
   Ill.: (c) Templegate Publishers, 1958. Reprinted with permis-
   sion of the publishers:
     A Marian Liturgy.

    <u>2) Previously uncopyrighted material:</u>

Rev. Lawrence D. Albertson....615
Rev. Joseph A. Appleyard, SJ..606
Rev. Robert A. Bagnato, SJ....Mass for an Apostolic Group
William Birmingham............213
Robert W. Cavanagh, SJ........616
John S. Chapman, SJ...........A Thanksgiving Liturgy (with Perko)
Rev. David L. Cooke, SJ.......609, An Experimental Liturgy for
                            Young Adults, A Wedding Liturgy
Clyde Crews..................617
Rev. Frank Dowling, SJ........618 (with Serrick)
Robert R. Dwelley, NSJ.......Liturgy of the Liberation of
                            the Soul
Rev. James L. Empereur, SJ....Introductions to individual sections
                            as noted, 607, 610, 803, An Experi-
                            mental Liturgy
Rev. Ernest C. Ferlita, SJ...619, 620

cf. also: "Liturgical Sources" at the end of A Marian Liturgy;
            p. 162.

....

INDEX OF SOURCES